Marriages

of

LOUSIA COUNTY

VIRGINIA

1766-1815

Compiled By:

Kathleen Booth Williams

Please direct all correspondence and orders to:

www.southernhistoricalpress.com
or
SOUTHERN HISTORICAL PRESS, Inc.
PO BOX 1267
375 West Broad Street
Greenville, SC   29601
southernhistoricalpress@gmail.com

ISBN #0-89308-881-1

Printed in the United States of America

FOREWORD

Louisa, 40 miles northwest of Richmond, was separated in 1742 from Hanover, which was taken in 1720/1 from New Kent. New Kent, in turn, was taken in 1654 from York, which was formerly named Charles River. Charles River was one of the eight original shires formed in 1634, the name being changed to York in 1642/3. (A Hornbook of Virginia History pp. 14, 16, 20).

Louisa was named in honor of Louisa, daughter of King George II, King of England. She was later wife of Frederick V, King of Denmark. (Colonial Virginia pp. 145-155).

When Louisa was formed, St. Martin's Parish was divided, that part lying in Louisa becoming Fredericksville Parish. In 1762 this Parish was divided and Trinity Parish was formed. (Fredericksville Parish Register 1742-1787).

Though Louisa County was formed in 1742, the Marriage Register does not begin until 1766, and Ministers' Returns begin in 1781.

The marriages herein contained, 1766-1815, were copied from the Marriage Registers for Louisa County, 1766-1861, found in the Virginia State Library, Richmond, Virginia, and such marriages from The Douglas Register as the Rev. William Douglas performed in Louisa County through 1815.

In the old records family names were often spelled several different ways. In using this book, therefore, the consultant should look for all possible variations.

In that era marriages were authorized by 'bond' and by 'banns'. Bonds were registered at the Court House of the county in which the bride lived. Banns were registered in the Church Register. Having banns published was the cheaper way. We feel that more marriages were performed than existent records show. Note how few marriages are recorded in 1766 and in 1777.

Gratitude is expressed to the librarians at the Virginia State Library and to Mr. L. A. Keller, Clerk of Louisa County Court, for their courtesy and help.

This book is offered hoping to help those interested in families of this area.

Kathleen Booth Williams

Mrs. E. Burton Williams
2702 Russell Road
Alexandria, Virginia

MARRIAGES OF LOUISA COUNTY, VIRGINIA

1766 - 1815

1 August 1799. Bandoine _____ and Anah Tuggle. Married by Rev. William Baskett. Ministers' Returns p 372

1 October 1799. Thomas ADAMS and Lucey Dickerson. Sur. Thomas Dickerson. Married 3 October by Rev. Richard Pope. p 90

13 September 1778. John ADKERSON and Elizabeth Shelton, dau. of Peter Shelton. Sur. John Nelson. Wit. David Shelton and John Saunders. p 11

23 December 1784. Abraham AILSTOCK and Isabel Ratcliff. Married by Rev. William Douglas. The Douglas Register p 23

5 November 1812. John AILSTOCK and Usley Ailstock. Sur. Absolm Ailstock. Married 7 November by Rev. William Cooke. p 149

9 February 1796. Watson ALCOCK and Elizabeth Walker. Sur. James Poindexter. Wit. John Bow. p 74

1 April 1802. Rev. Archibald ALEXANDER and Janetta Waddel, dau. of J. A. Waddel. Sur. James G. Waddell. Wit. William Calhoon. Married 6 April by Rev. William Calhoon. p 101

12 March 1782. Drury ALFORD and Betsey Cannon, dau. of Elizabeth Cannon. Sur. William Cannon. Wit. John Price and Richard Johnson. Married 13 March by Rev. William Douglas. p 19

2 March 1779. Jacob ALFORD and Nancy Hunter, dau. of Stephen Hunter. Sur. Rev. William Douglas. Wit. John Hunter and Hansel Alford. p 12

9 December 1805. John ALFRED and Nancey Hunter. Sur. Stephen Hunter. p 118

25 August 1812. David ALLEN and Ann F. Dabney. Sur. William Whitton. Wit. D. Dickenson. p 148

25 December 1780. David ALLEN and Lucy Gardner. Married by Rev. William Douglas. The Douglas Register p 20

11 November 1782. John ALLEN and Ann Sims. Sur. Micajah Sims. p 21

31 July 1793. John ALLEN and Patsy Chewning. Joseph
Chewning gives consent for Patsy. Sur. John Glenn.
Wit. Mare Chewning and William Chewning. (Patcy
Tuneing is also on the bond.) Married 1 August by Rev.
John Lasley. p 62

10 September 1814. William ALLEN and Elizabeth Morris.
Sur. John Morris. Married by Rev. John Lasley. p 156

2 October 1784. Thomas ALMAND, Jr. and Mary Sansum,
dau. of Elijah Sansum. Sur. Bartholomew Warren. Wit.
Asa Sims and John Cosby. Thomas is son of Thomas
Almand, Sr. p 26

24 October 1812. John ALMOND and Patsey Tudor. Sur.
Arthur Mann. Married 25 October by Rev. Claibourn
Walton. p 149

1 June 1795. Thomas ALMOND and Martha Tuter. Sur.
Bartholomew Warren. See Thomas Almond. p 71

4 June 1795. Thomas ALMOND and Martha Juter. Married by Rev. Martin Walton. See Thomas Almond.
Ministers' Returns p 366

22 June 1807. William ALMOND and Mildred Burgess,
Milley, over 21 years of age. Sur. John D. Watkins.
p 125

20 October 1808. Wyatt ALMOND and Susanna Ware. Sur.
Dudley Ware. p 131

16 May 1791. Benjamin ALVINSON and Fanny Rowe. Lucy
Rowe gives consent for Fanny. Sur. Thomas Johnson.
p 54

23 December 1793. Alexander ANDERSON and Lucy
Thomson, dau. of Marey Thompson. Sur. James Poindexter. Wit. Samuel J. Winston, Samuel Harris and Peter
Crutchfield. Lucy also written Lucy Thompson on the
bond. p 65

10 April 1770. Bartlelott ANDERSON and Frances Dick-
inson, dau. of Griffith Dickason. Sur. John Watson.
Wit. Hickason Cosby Dickason, Robert Dickason and
John Hawkins, Jr. p 2

5 September 1773. Benjamin ANDERSON and Sarah Johnson,
dau of David Johnson. Sur. William Jackson. Wit.
William Johnson and Ann Jackson. Benjamin is of
Albemarle County. Married 7 September by Rev.
William Douglas. p 7

2 July 1802. Francis ANDERSON and Lucy Phillips, over 21 years of age. Sur. Richard Phillips. p 101

6 October 1803. Garland ANDERSON and Mary Minor. Sur. Peter Minor. p 108

19 January 1807. John ANDERSON and Nancey Lasley, under age, dau. of John Lasley. Sur. William Boyd. Wit. Mary H. Lasley and Cynthy Holland. p 124

3 May 1772. Matthew ANDERSON and Elizabeth Anderson, dau. of Richard Anderson. Sur. John Nelson. Wit. Susannah Goodwin and Ann Longmire. p 5

29 October 1792. Matthew ANDERSON and Sarah Farrar. Sur. Stephen Farrar. p 60

10 August 1767. Nathaniel ANDERSON and Elizabeth Carr. Sur. John Carr. p 1

6 January 1801. Nicholas M. ANDERSON and Salley Bullock, dau. of David Bullock. Sur. Robert Thomson. Wit. Thomas Winston. Married 8 January by Rev. Richard Pope. p 96

27 April 1780. Richard ANDERSON and Caty Fox. Sur. John Fox. Married by Rev. William Douglas who says Col. Richard Anderson and Catherine Fox. p 14

23 October 1799. Richard ANDERSON and Milley Waddy, dau. of William Waddy. Sur. Nicholas M. Anderson. Wit. W. Thompson and John Thompson, Jr. p 90

12 June 1776. Turner ANDERSON and Susanna Daniel, asked only. Married by Rev. William Douglas. The Douglas Register p 17

17 December 1804. John ANDREW and Nancey Riddy, over 21 years of age. Sur. William Riddy. p 113

22 October 1789. Nathaniel ANTHONY and Nancy Keen. Sur. Zachariah Edwards. Wit. George Matlock and William Waddy. p 47

14 August 1802. William ANTHONY and Elenor B. Gentry, over 21 years of age, dau. of Mary Gentry. Sur. Stanley Alvis. Wit. William Perkins, David Kersey and J. L. Walton. p 102

22 March 1796. William APPLEBY and Martha Foster. Sur. Thomas Christmas. Married by Rev. Martin Walton. p 76

15 February 1790. James ARMSTRONG and Lucy Watson.
Sur. John Bailey. Wit. Lucinda Bailey. p 49

7 January 1800. John ARMSTRONG and Frankey Lefaun.
William Lefaun gives consent for Frankey. Sur. William Armstrong. Wit. David Hambleton and Elizabeth
Hambleton. Married 10 January by Rev. Martin
Walton. p 92

23 January 1809. John ARMSTRONG and Susanna M. Mann.
Sur. Thomas Mann. Married 1 February by Rev. John
Lasley. p 133

11 April 1811. John ARMSTRONG and Sally Gray (Sarah),
over 21 years of age. Sur. John Ware. p 143

4 October 1811. John B. ARMSTRONG and Amey Duke, dau.
of Hardin Duke. Sur. Garland Duke. p 145

23 February 1778. Lancelot ARMSTRONG and Mary Bourn,
dau. of Stephen Bourn of St. Martin's Parish. Sur.
John Lea. Wit. Richard Paulett. Lancelot is of
Trinity Parish. Married by Rev. Willian Douglas. p 11

12 July 1793. Lanslot ARMSTRONG and Elizabeth
McAllister. Sur. James Byars. Married 14 July by Rev.
Martin Walton who spells the name Larencelott. p 62

2 November 1782. William ARMSTRONG and Mary Nuckolds,
dau. of Keziah Nuckolls. Sur. Thomas Nuckolds. Wit.
William Nuckolls and James Nuckolls. Married 14
November by ⁿev. William Douglas. p 21

8 October 1787. William ARMSTRONG and Ann Ward, dau.
of William Ward. Sur. Reuben Thacker. Wit. Thomas
Gardner and William Tate. p 36

25 October 1779. David ARNETT and Mary Shackleford.
Sur. James Arnett. Married 28 October by Rev.
William Douglas. p 13

6 October 1783. James ARNETT and Sally Burrus.
Samuel Brockman is her guardian. Ann Linney gives
consent for Sally. Sur. William Richardson. Wit.
John Henderson and James Richardson. Married 10
October, no Minister's name given. p 23

8 August 1791. James ARNETT and Margarett Linney.
Sur. John Poindexter, Jr. p 55

13 December 1803. James ARNETT and Mary Emley
Robinson. Sur. James Robinson. p 109

2 November 1792. Lasly ARNETT and Frances Smith. Sur. Nathan Smith. p 60

14 December 1807. Thomas ARNETT and Matilda Cole. Sur. Armistead Cole. p 126

11 December 1781. William ARNETT and Moley Graves, dau. of Rice Graves. Sur. David Arnett. Wit. William White. Married 27 December by Rev. William Douglas. p 18

1 August 1791. William ARNETT and Mary Ann McGehee, dau. of James McGehee. Sur. John Graves. Wit. Richard McGehee. Married by Rev. William Douglas. p 55

8 September 1800. Zachariah ARNETT and Nancey Beadles. Sur. James Beadles. p 94

13 December 1803. Aaron ARNOLD and Louisa Pettus. Sur. William Cooke. p 109

9 January 1797. Hezekiah ARNOLD and Crosby C. Luck. Sur. John Lasley. Wit. Garland Dickerson and John Steward. Married 17 January by Rev. James Tolleson. p 80

19 December 1791. James ARNOLD and Nancey Lumsden, of full age, dau. of George Lumsden. Sur. William Lumsden. Wit. Henry Lumsden. Married 22 December by Rev. John Waller. p 57

9 January 1775. John ARNOLD and Barbary Pettus, dau. of William Pettus. Sur. Garrett Minor. Wit. Thomas Minor and William Arnold, Jr. p 9

14 November 1785. Lindsay ARNOLD and Elizabeth Davis (Betsy), dau. of Anna Davis. Sur. Jeduthan Davis. Wit. William Arnold and John Davies. p 30

11 October 1773. William ARNOLD and Susan Tate. Married by Rev. William Douglas. The Douglas Register p 14

24 October 1771. Elkanak ATKINS and Sally Austine. Married by Rev. William Douglas. The Douglas Register p 12

19 December 1810. Gerrard ATKINS and Rebecca McGehee, under 21 years of age, dau. of James McGehee, Sr. Sur. William Arnett. p 142

21 July 1808. Hezekiah ATKINS and Mary Bibb, 21 years of age. Sur. William Bibb. p 130

11 June 1795. Spencer ATKINS and Rebecca Yancey. Sur.
Reubin Grady. Wit. Susanna Atkins. Spencer is son of
Joseph Atkins. p 72

6 November 1783. John AUSTIN and Lucy Shelton, dau. of
Peter Shelton. Sur. Austin Hunter. Wit. George Hunter.
p 23

14 May 1793. Bolding BADGET and Elizabeth Ryan, dau. of
Philip Ryan. Sur. John Ryan. Married 16 May by Rev.
Martin Walton. p 62

8 January 1787. John BADGETT and Ann Tyler. Elizabeth
Johnson gives consent for Ann. Sur. Thomas Gardner.
Wit. Thomas Badget and Jemima Gardner. p34

10 December 1787. Thomas BADGET and Nancey Timberlake,
dau. of Philip Timberlake. Sur. John Badget. Wit.
John Tilford. p 37

12 January 1789. James BAGBY and ____ _____. Sur.
Stephen Terry. p 43

15 July 1786. John BAILEY and Lucinda Goldsmith.
Sur. William Goldsmith. p 33

14 November 1815. Nathaniel BAILEY and Mary Crank.
Sur. David Tisdale. Wit. Thomas Chewning. Married
by Rev. Claibourn Walton. p 159

6 May 1780. Thomas BAILEY and Nancy Gentry. Sur.
Nicholas Gentry. Married 7 May by Rev. William
Douglas. p 15

16 August 1791. Barnard BAKER and Nancy Anderson,dau.
of Bartlett Anderson. Sur. Matthew Mickie. Wit.
Nathaniel Seargeant and Jesse Chewning. Barnard also
written Barney W. Baker on the bond. Married by Rev.
John Waller. p 55

3 January 1797. Cleavears BAKER and Mary Mills, dau.
of William Mills. Sur. Thomas Swift. Wit. William
Mills, Jr. p 79

12 February 1781. John BAKER and Nancy Harris. Sur.
William Harris. Married by Rev. William Douglas.
p 17

24 September 1789. Joshua BAKER and Susanna Freeman.
Sur. Joseph Johnson. p 46

12 November 1807. Martin BAKER and Catharine Woodger.
Sur. Thomas Woodger. Married 13 November by Rev. John
Lasley. p 126

27 September 1815. Newel BAKER and Annis Lipscomb.
Sur. Martin Baker. Wit. John Sims. Married 30
September by Rev. William Cooke. p 159

28 January 1804. Newell BAKER and Susanna Mansfield,
dau. of William Mansfield. Sur. Robert Harris, Jr.
Wit. John Mansfield. p 110

10 August 1780. Overton BAKER and Molley Green. Married by Rev. William Douglas. The Douglas Register
p 20

17 January 1812. Samuel BAKER and Mary G. Fuqua, dau.
of William Fuqua. Sur. Thomas Baker. Married 23
January by Rev. William Cooke. p 146

10 February 1791. Thomas BAKER and Milley Gentry.
Sur. John Smith. Married 11 February by Rev. John
Lasley. p 53

16 November 1798. William BAKER and Jane Mansfield,
dau. of William Mansfield. Sur. Martin Sharp. Wit.
Elijah Dickinson. Married 22 November by Rev. William
Cooke. p 86

9 February 1792. Zachariah BALEY and Nancey Chewning,
dau. of William Chewning. Sur. Thomas Chewning. Wit.
John Poindexter. p 57

4 February 1806. George BANKS and Jemima Ann Overton,
dau. of Col. John Overton. Sur. Gerard Banks. Wit.
Eliza Bacon. p 120

19 June 1809. Thomas BARBEE and Alice B. Winston, of
lawful age. James Winston makes affadavit as to Alice's
age. Sur. John H. Winston. p 136

19 August 1814. John W. BARKER and Mary M. Meriwether.
Sur. John Brockman. p 155

13 January 1780. James BARLOW and Lucy Edwards. Sur.
Henry Edwards. Married by Rev. William Douglas who says
James is of Albemarle County. p 14

19 July 1804. Barrett BARNETT and Nancey Payne, dau. of
J. Payne. Sur. Richard Payne. Married 26 July by Rev.
William Baskett. p 112

4 June 1810. Peter S. BARRET and Matilda W. Pendleton, dau. of Henry Pendleton. Sur. James D. Turner. Married 7 June by Rev. William Cooke who says Barrett. p 139

5 November 1770. Charles BARRETT, Jr. and Elizabeth Clough. J. Templeton, her guardian, consents for Elizabeth. On the permission is 'Cluff'. Sur. John Nelson. Wit. John Marshall and George Pottie. p 3

19 April 1808. Charles BARRETT and Ann M. Johnson, dau. of Thomas Johnson, Sheriff, deceased. Sur. John W. Barrett. Wit. Thomas Johnson. Married 21 April by Rev. William Cooke who says Ann Meriwether Johnson. p 129

15 December 1806. Peter S. BARRETT and Sally F. Kimbrough, niece of Robert Yancey, who is her guardian. Sur. Charles Barrett. Wit. D. Yancey. p 123

18 December 1803. Robert BARRETT, Jr. and Nancey Bullock, (Ann), dau. of David T. Bullock. Sur. Edward Garland. Wit. Joseph Teary. p 109

12 September 1783. James BATES and Hithie Serjeant. Married by Rev. William Douglas. The Douglas Register. p 23

13 November 1793. Moses BATES and Elizabeth Garth. Sur. William Price. Married 14 November by Rev. Richard Pope. p 63

11 July 1796. Thomas BATES and Nancy Groom. Sur.Joel Parish. p76

25 July 1780. Shadrach BATTLES and Dolly Moss. Married by Rev. William Douglas. The Douglas Register p 20

25 April 1778. Joseph BAYNHAM and Keziah Davis. Sur. George Lumsden. p 11

29 May 1778. James BEADLES and Jane Daniel. Sur. Charles Daniel, Jr. p 11

8 May 1809. William BEADLES and Susan Lipscomb. Sur. John Lipscomb. Wit. Thomas Cole. James Beadles gives consent for William. p 135

24 October 1810. Robert BEARD and Sarah P. Smith, dau. of William Smith. Sur. N. Tarbet. p 141

21 May 1812. John BEAVER and Betsey Johnson, dau. of Thomas Johnson. Sur. Thomas Johnson, Jr. Wit. Jean Johnson. p 147

12 June 1782. Samuel BEAVER and Elizabeth Hopkins. Sur. John Beaver. p 20

15 April 1796. George BELL and Nancey Southerland. Sur. Joseph Southerland. Wit. William G. Poindexter. Married 19 April by Rev. William Lasley. p 76

4 March 1791. Robert BELL and Sarah Henson. Sur. Samuel Henson. Married 6 March by Rev. John Lasley. p 53

29 July 1805. John BELLOMY and Fanny Jones. Sur. James Bellomy. p 116

22 October 1792. William BELLOMY and Sarah Robards. Sur. Morris Robards. p 59

20 June 1782. Samuel BEVER and Elizabeth Timberlake. Married by Rev. William Douglas. The Douglas Register p 22

3 August 1790. Benjamin BIBB and Agnes Tate. Sur. Uriah Tate. Wit. James Poindexter. p 50

25 April 1788. Charles BIBB and Ann Humble, of age. She has resided in the County for a month or more. Sur. Absolum Tyler. Wit. Thomas Johnson. Married 29 April by Rev. William Douglas who says Annie Umbles. p 40

20 December 1783. James BIBB and Nancy Walke, dau. of Peter Walke. Sur. William Bigger, Jr. Wit. Thomas Green and James Arnet. (See James Bibb and Nancy Walker) p 24

21 December 1783. James BIBB and Nancy Walker. No Minister's name is given. (See James Bibb and Nancy Walke). Ministers' Returns p 360

22 December 1808. James BIBB and Nancey Kennon. Sur. John Kennon. Married 27 December by Rev. John Lasley. p 132

28 September 1779. John BIBB and Sarah Thomason, dau. of George Thomasson. Sur. Henry Bibb. Wit. Richard Thomasson. Married 29 September by Rev. William Douglas. p 13

23 October 1799. John BIBB and Sarah McGehee. James McGehee gives consent for Sarah. Sur. Robert Groom. Wit. William L. McGehee. p 90

14 December 1811. John BIBB and Polly Seargeant, dau. of John Seargeant. Sur. William Seargeant. Wit. John Poindexter, Jr. Married 22 December by Rev. John Lasley. p 145

9 March 1812. Robert BIBB and Sarah Thomason. Sur. Robert Thompson. p 147

3 December 1787. Thomas BIBB and Elizabeth Carpenter, dau. of John Carpenter. Sur. John Bibb. Wit. John Poindexter, Joseph Poindexter and Charles Slaughter. Married 4 December by Rev. William Douglas. p 37

30 November 1808. Thomas BIBB and Rebecca T. Harris. Sur. Richard McGehee. Wit. James Bibb. p 131

23 December 1808. Wright BIBB and Sally Morris, dau. of George Morris. Sur. Charles M. Hughes. p 133

2 April 1799. Humphrey BICKLEY and Agnes Crews. William and Usle Crews give consent for Agnes. Sur. William Crews or John Crews. Wit. Tibby Fowler. Married 3 April by Rev. John Lasley. p 88

8 May 1798. Joseph BICKLEY and Polley Henley. Sur. William G. Poindexter. Wit. Wilson Henley. Married 9 May by Rev. Reuben Ford who says Joseph Bickley, Bachelor and Polley Hendley, Spinster. p 84

22 July 1799. Macon BIGGAR and Christian Poindexter. Married by Rev. William Douglas. (See Macon Bigger) The Douglas Register p 19

20 July 1799. Macon BIGGER and Christian Gizage.Sur. John Poindexter. (See Macon Biggar). p 12

14 June 1779. John BIGGERS and Mildred Ferguson. Sur. John Maddeson. Wit. Sydnor Cosby. p 12

15 April 1794. John BIRD and Nancy Thacker, dau. of Mary Thacker. Sur. William Thacker. Wit. William Clarke and William Johnson. p 67

19 September 1771. George BLACKBURN and Prudence Berry. James Mitchell, father-in-law and guardian of Prudence, consents. Sur. William James Thurston. p 4

1 December 1787. Charles BLUNT and Mary Waters Pettus, of age. Sur. John Waters Pettus. Married 2 December by Rev. William Douglas. p 37

10 June 1785. George BOND and Sarah Chase. Married by Rev. William Douglas. The Douglas Register p 24

19 April 1813. Thomas BOND and Polley Hinchie. Sur. Richard Thompson. Married 4 June by Rev. William Cooke. p 152

21 August 1787. William BOND and Elizabeth Cole, over 21 years of age, dau. of Joseph Cole. Sur. Richard Cole. Wit. Zinvie Tate. Married 23 August by Rev. William Douglas. p 36

4 July 1788. Wright BOND and Frances Grady. Sur. William Grady. Married 6 July by Rev. William Douglas. p 40

12 January 1795. Uel BOULWARE and Mary Ragland. Sur. John R. Ragland. p 70

8 December 1794. David BOURNE and Hannah Bourne, dau. of Stephen Bourne. Sur. Zachariah Pulliam. Wit. John Diggs. p 69

28 December 1801. John BOW and Matilda Bickley, (also written Caroline Matilda Bickley on the bond). Sur. Joseph Lasley. Wit. John Lasley and David Draper. Married by Rev. John Lasley who says Caroline Matilda Bickley. p 100

12 March 1796. Augustine BOWLES and Elizabeth W. Isbell. Joseph Isbell gives consent for Elizabeth. Sur. Robert T. Isbell. Married 17 March by Rev. Martin Walton. p 75

20 December 1800. John BOWLES and Peggy Anderson. Sur. Nathan Anderson. Wit. John Anderson. Married 24 December by Rev. Duke W. Hullum. p 96

9 October 1797. George BOXLEY and Catharine Barkley. Sur. Patrick Barkley. p 82

14 April 1789. John S. BOXLEY and Mary W. Barclay. Sur. James Dickinson. Married 18 April by Rev. William Douglas. p45

20 December 1814. Joseph BOXLEY and Mary H. McGehee, dau. of W. McGehee. Sur. John C. Boxley. Wit. William McGehee, Jr. Married 23 December by Rev. William Cooke. p 156

17 October 1803. Pallison BOXLEY and Susanna Dickinson, over 21 years of age. Sur. James C. Dickinson. p 108

10 August 1807. Thomas BOXLEY and Elizabeth Broaddus. Sur. Pallison Boxley. p 125

23 December 1799. Thomas BOYD and Elizabeth Sims. Sur. Benjamin Sims. Married 26 December by Rev. John Lasley. p 91

17 December 1800. William BOYD and Mary Timberlake. Philip Timberlake gives consent for Mary. Sur. John Timberlake. Married 23 December by Rev. John Lasley. p 96

21 April 1781. Butler BRADBURN and Elizabeth Harris, dau. of William Harris. Sur. William Bradburn. Wit. Robert Harris and Samuel Harris. p 17

7 January 1782. William BRADBURN and Mary Johnson. Sur. William Harris. p 19

16 June 1808. John BRAGG and Susanna Turner (Susan). Sur. James D. Turner. p 129

29 December 1792. Richard BRAGG and Milley Reynolds. Sur. William Reynolds. p 61

13 July 1772. George BRAIKENRIDGE and Sarah Jerdone, dau. of Sarah Jerdone. Sur. John Nelson. Wit. George Pottie who gives consent for George. p 5

22 December 1797. Ludlow BRAMHAM and Sarah Michie. Sur. James Michie. Wit. John Michie. p 83

3 August 1793. Ambrose BRANHAM and Susanna S. Johnson. Sur. Benjamin Branham. Married 5 September by Rev. John Lasley who says Susanna Slater Johnson. p 62

26 March 1795. Nathaniel BRANHAM and Patty Napper. Sur. John Dalton. Wit. John Downing. Married by Rev. John Lasley who says Brenham. p 71

25 February 1771. Reynold BRIGHTWELL and Drucilla Allmand. Sur. Thomas Allmand. p 4

8 June 1774. Lyddall BRITON (?) and Elizabeth Jackson, dau. of Thomas Jackson who is surety. Wit. Nelson Anderson and Thomas Jackson, Jr. p 8

30 May 1809. John BROCKMAN and Ann Meriwether. Sur.
Garland Anderson. Married 31 May by Rev. Robert Jones
who says <u>Mrs</u>. Ann Meriwether. 'Mrs' is not on the
bond. p <u>135</u>

8 February 1813. Thomas BRONAUGH and Judith Hart, dau.
of Malcolm Hart, Sr. Sur. John Hart. Wit. Malcolm
Hart, Minor. Married 24 February by Rev. William
Cooke. p 151

14 November 1791. William BRONAUGH and Peggey BRONAUGH.
Sur. Samuel Bronaugh. p 56

2 August 1791. Aaron BROOCKMAN and Lydia Porter. Eben
Porter gives consent for Lydia. Sur. James Porter.
p 55

22 August 1803. Charles BROOKS and Elizabeth Harris,
(Betsey), dau. of Patrick Harris. Sur. Edmund
Badgett. Wit. Pole Harris. p 107

5 October 1801. James BROOKS and Cary Adams, over 21
years of age, dau. of Susanna Adams. Sur. Thomas Adams.
Wit. Sarah Clark. Married by Rev. Richard Pope. p 99

29 October 1789. John BROOKS and Mary Knott, dau. of
Robert and Elizabeth Knott. Sur. Jacob Martin. Wit.
Jinea Stears, John Gillman, John Brooks and John
Hanes. p 47

21 December 1787. Thomas BROOKS and Judah Badget.
(Also written <u>Judith</u> on the bond), dau. of Sarah
Badget. Each is 21 years of age. Sur. John Badget.
Wit. Thomas Johnson, John Brooks and Thomas Badget.
p 38

6 June 1784. William BROOKS and Elizabeth Jacobs.
Married by Rev. William Douglas. The Douglas
Register. p 23

17 May 1781. Armistead BROWN and Sally Daniel. Sur.
James Daniel. Married by Rev. William Douglas. p 17

16 May 1785. Charles BROWN and Heneriter Arnett,
sister of James Arnett who is surety. Wit. Francis
Arnett. Married 17 May by Rev. William Douglas who
says <u>Henrietta</u>. p 28

2 February 1813. Edward BROWN and Malinda Edwards, dau.
of Gravatt Edwards. Sur. John Stewart (also written
John Stuart). Married by Rev. Claibourn Walton. p 150

18 February 1812. John BROWN and Salley Hinchey, over
21 years of age, dau. of Bartlett Hinchey. Sur.
Richard W. Thompson. Wit. Overton Hinchey. p 147

1 July 1806. Miller BROWN and Susanna C. Thompson,
(also written Susanna Chiles Thomson), over 21 years
of age, dau. of Joseph Thomson. Sur. Joseph Thomson,
Jr. Wit. Salley J. Grubbs and Ann W. Clopton. Miller
Brown is of Hanover County. p 121

17 March 1798. Robert T. BROWN and Elizabeth Crenshaw.
Sur. David Crenshaw. Married 27 March by Rev. Hezekiah
Arnold. p 84

8 January 1810. Thomas BROWN and Salley H. Edwards.
Sur. Ivy Edwards. Wit. Charles Yancy. p 138

30 October 1781. William BROWN and Dorothea Long.
Married by Rev. William Douglas. The Douglas
Register p 21

14 October 1795. John BROWNING and Mary Foster. Sur.
William Foster. p 73

26 December 1793. John BRYANT and Elizabeth Phillips,
niece of William Phillips. Sur. Nuckolls Johnson.
Married 1 January, 1794 by Rev. Richard Pope. p 65

4 February 1778. David BULLOCK and Susanna Moore, 21
years of age. Sur. John Moore, Jr. Wit. Thomas
Johnson, Sr. Married by Rev. William Douglas. p 11

11 February 1782. David BULLOCK and Jane Terry, dau.
of James Terry. Sur. John Nuckolls. Wit. Stephen
Terry and Thomas Terrell. Married 12 February by Rev.
William Douglas. p 19

24 December 1796. Joseph BULLOCK and Nancy Edwards,
Sur. Reuben Edwards. Married 25 December by Rev.
John Lasley. p 79

1 March 1794. Anderson BUNCH and Adney Bunch, dau. of
Pouncey Bunch. Sur. Paul Bunch. Wit. Nathaniel Bunch
and Thomas Bunch. Married 4 March by Rev. John Lasley.
p 66

22 February 1803. Anderson BUNCH and Barbara Crawford,
dau. of John Crawford. Sur. William Lawrence. Married
23 February by Rev. John Lasley. p 105

26 June 1787. Anthony BUNCH and Mary Bunch, 26 years of
age, dau. of Samuel Bunch. Sur. George Bunch. Wit.
Nathaniel Bunch. Married 28 June by Rev. John Lasley.
p 36

9 January 1792. Charles BUNCH and Mary Bellomy, dau of John Bellomy. Sur. William Bellomy. Wit. George Bunch. p 57

13 January 1806. David BUNCH and Elizabeth Wright, dau. of John Wright. Sur. Reuben Reynolds. p 119

15 July 1788. George BUNCH and Salley Sergeant, dau of William Sergeant. Sur. Martin Gentry. Wit. James Harris and John Harris. Married 18 July by Rev. John Lasley. p 40

23 January 1799. Jesse BUNCH and Elizabeth Pulliam. Sur. James Pulliam. Married 24 January by Rev. John Lasley. p 88

25 October 1808. Josiah BUNCH and Elizabeth Turner, dau. of Thomas Turner, Sr. Sur. Barnet D. Harris. Wit. James D. Turner. p 131

12 December 1793. Paul BUNCH and Mary Hancock, dau.of George Hancock. Sur. Thomas Bunch. Wit. Samuel McGraw. p 64

14 March 1814. Samuel BUNCH and Marina Arnett. Sur. Thomas Turner. p 155

22 April 1799. Suprey BUNCH and Nancey Sims. Sur. Benjamin Sims. Married 30 April by Rev. John Lasley. p 89

11 December 1811. Suprey BUNCH and Clarysy Bunch. Sur. Nicholas J. Poindexter. Wit. Samuel Bunch and David Bunch. p 145

12 September 1803. Walter BUNCH and Dycie Bunch. Sur. Pouncey Bunch. Married 15 September by Rev. John Lasley who says Dicie. p 107

30 October 1806. Henry M. BURNLEY and Ann Goodman, over 21 years of age. John Burnley, Sr. makes affadavit as to Ann's age. Sur. James Burnley, Sr. p 122

28 May 1794. James BURNLEY and Elizabeth Goodman, of age. Sur. Harden Duke. Wit. William Mills. p 67

13 December 1785. John BURNLEY and Susannah Crenshaw. Sur. James Duke. Married 15 December by Rev. William Douglas. p 30

25 February 1799. Moses BURNLEY and Polley Vest. Sur. John Vest. p 88

23 April 1811. Zachariah BURNLEY and Elizabeth Fox, over 21 years of age. Sur H. W. Burnley or Henry Burnley. Married 25 April by Rev. William Cooke. p 144

9 March 1812. Nathaniel BURRUS and Rebecca Massie. Sur. George Massie. p 147

7 November 1786. William BURTON and Molly Smith. Sur. Edward Smith. Married 10 November by Rev. John Lasley. p 34

1 May 1793. William BUSBY and Molley Lane. Sur. Jacob Lane. Married by Rev. Richard Pope. p 62

9 May 1803. Augustine BUTLER and Nancy Crews. Sur. Joel Crews. Married 10 May by Rev. John Lasley. p 106

1 January 1810. John BUTLER and Mary Tate. Sur. David Hall. Married 13 January by Rev. William Cooke. p 138

3 November 1795. Nathan BUTLER and Jane Bickley, 21 years of age, dau. of Sarah Haddock. Sur. Abisha Pemberton. Wlt. Charles Bickley and Christopher Butler. Married 4 November by Rev. John Lasley. p 73

1 May 1815. Patrick BUTLER and Milley White. Sur. Richard White. Wit. John White. Married by Rev. Claibourn Walton. p 158

29 August 1789. Peter BUTLER and Rhoda Sims. Sur. Austin Yeamans. Married 30 August by Rev. Charles Hopkins. p 46

10 December 1793. George BYARS and Rebecca Sims. Sur. Asa Sims. p 64

20 March 1809. John S. BYARS and Martha Terry, dau. of Stephen Terry. Sur. John Smith, Jr. Wit. James Terry. p 135

19 December 1782. James BYERS and Lovinia Smith. Married by Rev. William Douglas. The Douglas Register p 22

16 June 1804. John BYRD, Jr. and Henrietta Gibson, 21 years of age. Sur. John Cole. Wit. James Garland and Robert Garland. p 112

14 December 1795. Richard BYRD and Sally Carpenter, dau. of Philip Carpenter. Sur. Samuel Cole. Wit. James Hendrick. p 74

6 August 1806. Thomas BYRD and Lucy Bond, over 21 years of age. Sur. John Byrd. Wit. Micajah Clark, Jr. p 121

28 July 1797. Rev. William CALHOON and Elizabeth Waddel. James Waddel gives consent for Elizabeth. Sur. James G. Waddel. Married 5 August by Rev. James Waddel. p 81

7 April 1778. Daniel M. CALLA and Elizabeth Todd, dau. of John Todd. Sur. Joseph Thomson. Daniel M. Calla is also written Rev. Daniel McAlla on the bond. p 11

27 January 1807. Cleon M. CALLIS and Catharine Smith, dau. of William Smith. Sur. William O. Barrett. Wit. Daniel Ashton, Lynch Terrell, Thomas Hardin and Nathaniel Garland. Cleon, 21 years of age on 14 January 1807, is son of W. O. Callis. p 124

31 December 1788. Francis CAMPBELL and Nancey Barnett. Sur. James Barnett. Married 1 January 1789 by Rev. John Lasley. p 43

18 January 1810. George CARNALL and Betsey Chiles. Sur. Henry Chiles. Married by Rev. John Lasley who says Elizabeth. p 138

10 November 1813. Clifton CARPENTER and Mary W. Beadles. Sur. James Beadles. Married by Rev. William Y. Hiter. p 154

22 December 1797. Elijah CARPENTER and Elizabeth Byars. Sur. William Byars. p 83

18 December 1809. James CARPENTER and Susanna McGehee, under 21 years of age, dau. of James McGehee, Sr. Sur. Richard McGehee. p 137

13 September 1813. John CARPENTER and Ann Gibson. Sur. William Gibson. Married 16 September by Rev. William Cooke. p 153

13 March 1815. Joseph CARPENTER and Nancy Smith, dau. of George Smith. Sur. James Smith. p 157

10 December 1804. Joseph T. CARPENTER and Jane Southerland. Joseph Southerland gives consent for Jane. Sur. Benjamin M. Smith. Wit. Nancey Bell. Married 13 December by Rev. William Cooke who says Joseph H. Carpenter. p 113

13 December 1803. Pleasant CARPENTER and Patsey
Biggers, dau. of John Biggers. Sur. Joseph Carpenter.
Married 14 December by Rev. Duke W. Hullam. p 109

6 January 1808. Daniel F. CARR and Emily Terrell, dau.
of W. Terrell, Jr. Sur. Richmond Terrell. Wit:Elenor
Terrell. p 127

4 October 1781. Thomas CARROL and Mildred Walker.
Married by Rev. William Douglas. The Douglas
Register p 21

17 March 1815. John CARROLL and Mary Perkins, dau. of
Elizabeth Perkins. Sur. Hardin Perkins. Married by
Rev. John Lasley. p 157

19 June 1812. Samuel CARROLL and Bettsy Baker, dau. of
Susanna Nilton. Sur. Lewis F. Waller. Married 23 June
by Rev. John Lasley. p 148

8 November 1815. John CARVER and Elizabeth Sprouse,
dau. of James Sprouse. Sur. John Sprouse. Wit.
William R. Bellomy. p 159

13 July 1814. Benjamin CASH and Sally Faris. Sur.
William Faris. p 155

15 October 1790. Reuben CASON and Lucy McGehee, dau.
of John McGehee. Sur. Edward McGehee. Married 21
October by Rev. John Waller. p 51

8 April 1789. Nathaniel CAWLEY and Mary Holland, dau.
of George Holland. Sur. Michael Holland. Wit. Isbell
Holland. p 45

22 July 1788. Carter CHANDLER and Judith Young. Sur.
James Young. Married 24 July by Rev. William Douglas.
p 41

14 March 1796. George CHAMBERS and Elizabeth White.
Sur. Chapman White. p 75

29 August 1791. James CHAMBERS and Anne Roberson.
Sur. Richard Roberson. p 56

7 February 1797. Anderson CHASE and Franky Norman.
Sur. Archer Thacker. p 80

25 December 1790. William CHASE and Pasience Goodrige,
dau. of Ann Goodrige. Sur. Archelaus Thacker. Wit.
Annis Thacker. On the bond the name is also written
Pasience Goodrich. Married by Rev. William Douglas.
p 53

16 December 1790. Calis CHEWNING and Nancey Hubbard,
over 21 years of age. Sur. Butler Bradburn. Wit.
Alexander Anderson. Married by Rev. John Lasley. p 53

29 May 1783. George CHEWNING and Jeanie Bunch. Married
by Rev. William Douglas. The Douglas Register p 15

13 September 1802. Jesse CHEWNING and Polly Wash, dau.
of Will Wash. Sur. James Kennedy. Wit. John Crawford.
Married by Rev. John Lasley. p 102

18 September 1805. John CHEWNING and Nancey Tisdale.
Sur. Shirley Tisdale. Married by Rev. John Lasley.
p 116

18 December 1799. Reubin CHEWNING and Anne Dickason,
dau. of Robert Dickason. Sur. Jesse Chewning. Wit.
James Dickinson and Jonathan Dickinson, Jr. p 91

29 May 1811. Theophilus CHEWNING and Ann Elmore,
between 25 and 30 years of age. Charles Quarles makes
affadavit as to her age. Sur. William Osborne. p 144

7 January 1800. Thomas CHEWNING and Betsey Crank,
over 21 years of age, dau. of Henry Crank. Sur. Thomas
Mann, Jr. Married 8 January by Rev. John Lasley. p 92

29 December 1804. Garland CHILES and Hannah Edwards
Johnson. Sur. Richard Johnson. Married 30 December
by Rev. John Lasley. p 114

20 December 1785. James CHILES and Susannah Graves.
Rice Graves gives consent for Susannah. Sur. Richard
Graves. Wit. James Daniel and William Graves. p 30

1 March 1775. Thomas CHILES and Susanna Kimbrow.
Robert Kimbrow, her brother, makes affadavit Susanna
is of age. Sur. John Lipscomb. Wit. Joseph McGehee
and Robert Kimbrough. p 10

10 November 1800. William CHILES and Elizabeth
Cawthorn. William White makes affadavit Elizabeth is
over 21 years of age. Sur. William G. Poindexter.
Wit. John White, Jr. Married by Rev. Richard Ferguson.
Returned 19 August 1801. p 96

29 March 1806. Suprey CHISHOLM and Susanna C.Chisholm,
dau. of Thomas Chisholm. Sur. John R. Chisholm. Wit.
Hugh Chisholm. p 120

6 October 1794. John CHRISTMAS and Ann Jackson. Sur.
Charles Jackson. Married 9 October by Rev. Martin
Walton. p 68

28 November 1782. Simon CHRISTOPHER and Ann Mitchell.
Sur. Daniel Lane. Married 1 December by Rev. William
Douglas. p 21

12 July 1810. Christopher CLARK and Elizabeth Hope.
Married by Rev. John Lasley. Ministers' Returns.
p 385

8 October 1798. James CLARK and Aylse Ragland. Sur.
John R. Ragland. Married 11 October by Rev. John
Lasley who says Aylie . p 85

10 December 1770. Micajah CLARK and Luranna Johnson.
(Luraney is also on the bond). Sur. James Pulliam.
p 3

11 February 1811. Reuben CLARK and Jane Spanis. Sur.
Jesse Humphrey. p 143

17 November 1803. William CLARKE and Sally M.
Anderson. Sur. Nicholas M. Anderson. Wit. William
Kerr. Married 20 November by Rev. William Baskett.
p 109

7 May 1798. John CLAYBROOK and Sarah Overton. Sur.
Samuel Overton, Jr. Married 10 May by Rev. William
Cooke. p 84

2 September 1799. Arthur CLAYTON and Polly P. White,
dau. of William White. Sur. William Harwood. Wit.
Eli Cauthorn and A. C. White. p 90

20 October 1790. John COATS and Sally Perry Garth.
Sur. William Price, Jr. Married 21 October by Rev.
John Lasley. p 51

19 November 1783. Robert COBBS and Ann Gizage Poindexter. Sur. John Poindexter. Married by Rev.
William Douglas who says Cobb. p 24

17 April 1802. William COCKE and Nancy Turner, dau.
of Lewis Turner. Sur. Nathaniel Holland. Wit.
Peyton Bailey and Jack F. Cock. p 101

19 March 1808. John COGIL and Nancey Duke, over 21
years of age, dau. of Cleveas Duke. Sur. Henry Alvis.
p 129

26 September 1792. William COGHILL and Barbary
Goodwin, dau. of Jane Goodwin. Sur. Hugh Goodwin.
Married 27 September by Rev. John Waller. p 59

4 October 1798. Armistead COLE and Nancy Harris, dau. of Nathan Harris. Sur. William Hollins. Wit. George Harris. p 85

22 December 1807. John COLE and Nancey Wharton, under 21 years of age, dau. of Samuel Wharton. Sur. James McAllister. Wit. James Bibb. John is over 21 years of age. p 127

8 October 1810. John COLE and Susan Gooch. Sur. Peter M. Daniel. p 140

27 December 1785. Richard COLE and Sarah Sansum. Sur. William Cole. Married 29 December by Rev. William Douglas. p 30

8 July 1803. Wasley COLE and Elizabeth McAllister. William McAllister gives consent for Elizabeth. Sur. James McAllister, Sr. (See Wesley Cole). p 107

Returns of 1 May 1804. Wesley COLE and Elisabeth McAllister. Married by Rev. Richard Ferguson. (See Wasley Cole). Ministers' Returns p 379

4 March 1809. William COLE and Sissa Cole. Sur. Samuel Cole. Wit. Oswald Gibson. p 134

14 January 1789. William COLE, Jr. and Salley Byars, dau. of Elizabeth Byars. Sur. Nathaniel Harris. Wit. James McAlester, William Hopkins and Fleming Thomason. William, Jr. is son of William Cole. Married 15 January by Rev. William Douglas. p 43

_____ 1791. Francis COLEMAN and Mary Garret Brook. Married by Rev. William Douglas. The Douglas Register. p 27

7 July 1794. Francis COLEMAN and Elizabeth R. Gordon. Sur. Jonathan Gordon. Wit. Nathaniel Gordon. p 67

22 August 1814. Hawes COLEMAN and Ann Overton, dau. of James Overton. Sur. James Beadles. Wit. Elizabeth Hall and Nelson Barrett. Married 26 August by Rev. William Cooke. p 155

19 May 1787. Spencer COLEMAN and Elizabeth Goodwin. Sur. Robert Goodwin. p 35

7 March 1767. William COLEMAN and Sarah Farish, dau. of Robert Farish. Sur. Henry Winslow. Wit. Tommy Farish, Letty Farish and John Timberlake. p 1

21 May 1800. Burwell COLLINS and Lucy Harris, of lawful age. Sur. Richard Luck. Married 25 May by Rev.
William Cooke. p 93

14 February 1803. John COLLINS and Sarah Fleming. Sur.
John Luck. Wit. Robert Fleming. p 105

25 February 1808. John L. COLLINS and Elizabeth
McGehee, dau. of W. McGehee. Sur. George McGehee.
Wit. James Tinsley. p 128

6 November 1790. Mordecai COLLINS and Susanna Robertson, 21 years of age. Sur. James Chalmers. Wit.
Thomas Johnson. Married by Rev. William Douglas. p 52

22 March 1813. Edward N. COOKE and Nancey Baker. Sur.
Oswell McGehee. Wit. Mary Baker. Married 25 March by
Rev. William Cooke. p 151

21 November 1803. Mordecai COOKE and Nancey McGehee,
dau. of Edward McGehee. Sur. George Lumsden. Wit.
Dabney McGehee. Married 23 November by Rev. William
Cooke. p 109

27 December 1813. James COOPER and Nancy Langford.
Each is over 21 years of age. Sur. Richard Langford.
Wit. Amy Crank. Married 28 December by Rev. John
Lasley. p 154

4 December 1810. Pleasant CORLEY and Nancy Rion, dau.
of Nancy and William Rion. Sur. Robert Rion. Wit.
Polly Rion. Married 11 December by Rev. William Cooke.
p 142

28 October 1797. William CORLEY and Frances S. Hanes.
Married by Rev. William Cooke. Ministers' Returns p 370

8 November 1810. William CORLEY and Salley Kersey.
Sur. David Sims. Wit. David Sims, Jr. Married 29 November by Rev. William Cooke. p 141

25 August 1797. Austin COSBY and Dianna Swift, dau. of
Mary Swift. Sur. Duke Cosby. Wit. Joseph Swift. p 81

13 December 1785. Charles COSBY and Elizabeth Smith.
Sur. William Smith. Wit. David Bullock. p 30

13 July 1795. Charles COSBY and Sarah Smith. Sur.
William Smith. Married 28 July by Rev. William Cooke,
who says Sally M. Smith. p 72

20 December 1792. Duke COSBY and Amelia Harris, dau. of
Robert Harris. Sur. John Toler. Wit. Austin Cosby and
Thomas Smith. Duke is son of Charles Cosby. p 60

1 March 1800. Edward Rice COSBY and Mary Boyd, dau. of
John Boyd. Sur. Nathaniel Bunch. Wit. Thomas Boyd.
Married 5 March by Rev. William Baskett. p 93

10 November 1795. Fortunatus COSBY and Mary Ann Fontaine.
Sur. Aaron Fontaine. Married by Rev. William Douglas
who says Fortunas. p 73

22 June 1782. Garland COSBY and Molley Poindexter.
Sur. Thomas Poindexter. Married 27 June by Rev. William Douglas. p 20

10 October 1780. Hickason COSBY and Ann Harris, dau. of
Archlaus Harris. Sur. Charles Wingfield. Wit. Byrd Hendrick. Married 13 October by Rev. William Douglas. p 15

26 December 1800. Joel COSBY and Polley Cole, dau. of
Samuel Cole. Sur. John Cole. Wit. Samuel Cole, Jr.
Married by Rev. Richard Ferguson. Return dated 19 Aug-
ust 1801. p 96

19 April 1781. Thomas COSBY and Elizabeth Watkins,
dau. of James Watkins. Sur. Samuel Cole. Wit. Archelaus Harris. Married 20 April by Rev. William Douglas.
p 17

26 October 1797. William COSBY and Frances Sharp. Sur.
David Smith. p 82

10 November 1806. William COSBY and Fanny Byrd, over
21 years of age. Sur. John Byrd, Jr. p 122

11 December 1815. John W. COWHERD and Anna R. Winston,
dau. of Joseph Winston. Sur. William Anderson. Wit.
P. J. Rawlins. John is son of Reuben Cowherd. Married
by Rev. William Y. Hiter. p 160

11 November 1782. Aaron CRANE and Susannah Veatch. Sur.
James Veatch. p 21

31 December 1794. William CRANK and Tabitha Poindexter.
Sur. James Poindexter. Married 1 January 1795 by Rev.
John Lasley. p 70

25 February 1782. Peter CRAWFORD and Betsey Shelton,
dau. of William Shelton. Sur. James Byars. Wit. Nancy
Shelton. Married 11 April by Rev. William Douglas.
p 19

16 August 1796. William CRAWFORD and Rhoda C. Yancey.
Sur. Joseph Kimbrough. p 77

3 January 1797. Joel CRENSHAW and Jane Swift (Jean),
dau. of Richard Swift. Sur. John Swift. Wit. Dinah
Swift. Married 5 January by Rev. William Cooke. p 79

3 November 1794. Nathan CRENSHAW and Frances Higgason,
dau. of Samuel Higgason. Sur. Benjamin C. West. Wit.
John Jackson, Benj. Claborn West and Jesse White. Married 4 November by Rev. Martin Walton. p 68

14 June 1774. Thomas CRENSHAW and Ann Crenshaw, dau.
of William Crenshaw. Sur. Charles Crenshaw. Wit.
David Crenshaw and Mary Crenshaw. p 8

29 January 1783. William CRENSHAW and Sarah Baker.
Sur. William Baker. Married 30 January by Rev. William
Douglas. p 22

19 July 1799. William CRENSHAW and Rietta Sanders.
Sur. John Sanders. Wit. Mercy Sanders. Married 23 July
by Rev. William Douglas. p 12

9 March 1772. Amsbe CREW and Lucy Stone. Sur. Benjamin Mosby. p 5

23 December 1815. Clark CREWS and Salley Gilbert, dau.
of John Gilbert, Sr. Sur. William Reynolds. Wit. Isham
Homes. p 160

1 February 1797. William CREWS and Winny Bunch, dau. of
Poley Bunch. Sur. Nathaniel Bunch. Married by Rev. John
Lasley. p 80

12 November 1805. William CREWS, Sr. and Susanna Rittenhouse. Sur. Richard Faris. Wit. Micajah Clark. p 117

15 July 1805. Oliver CROSS and Ann Michie. Sur. Robert
Michie. Married 16 July by Rev. John Lasley. p 116

2 April 1799. Stapleton CRUTCHFIELD and Elizabeth Lewis
Minor, dau. of Garritt Minor. Sur. Garrett Minor, Jr.
p 88

23 March 1797. Fredrick CULP and Mary Flannagan. Married by Rev. John Lasley. Ministers' Returns p 370

8 September 1775. John CURD and Ann Underwood. Married by Rev. William Douglas. The Douglas Register p 16

17 December 1792. Robert DABNEY and Elizabeth Christmas.
Ann Christmas gives consent for Elizabeth. Sur. Thomas
Jackson. Wit. Charles Jackson. p 60

20 January 1775. Samuel DABNEY and Jane Meriwether. Thomas Johnson, Jr. gives consent for each party. Sur. James Mickie. p 9

25 April 1792. William DABNEY and Sarah Watson, dau, of James Watson. Sur. Joseph Shelton. Wit. David Watson. p 58

31 October 1782. Bradley DALTON and Dolly Robertson. Married by Rev. William Douglas. The Douglas Register p 22

25 September 1779. David DALTON and Sarah Robinson. Sur. William Robinson. Married 27 September by Rev. William Douglas. p 13

14 May 1810. David DALTON and Frances Freeman. Sur. William Gibson. Wit. James Dobs. Married 17 May by Rev. John Lasley. p 139

28 December 1803. Robert DALTON and Suckey Hughes. Sur. William Hughes. p 110

21 August 1797. William DALTON and Rachael Thacker. Sur. Nathaniel Branham. Wit. Thomas Greene and John Dalton. p 81

5 March 1803. Richard A. DANDRIDGE and Fanny Anderson, dau. of Matthew Anderson. Sur. John Hargrave, Jr. Wit. Joseph Williams and James Cochran. Married 9 March by Rev. Charles Hopkins. p 105

10 May 1790. Jesse DANIEL and Frances A. Nelson. Sur. James Poindexter. p 50

2 February 1780. John DANIEL and Sarah Chiles. Sur. Turner Anderson. Married 3 February by Rev. William Douglas. p 14

8 October 1810. Peter M. DANIEL and Ann P. Gooch. Sur. Nicholas J. Poindexter. p 140

30 March 1789. William DANIEL and Mary Thomasson, of age. Sur. David Shelton. Wit. Samuel Thomasson and Richard Thomasson. (See William Daniel). p 44

30 March 1789. William DANIEL and Mary Thomas. Married by Rev. William Douglas. (See William Daniel). The Douglas Register p 25

30 May 1796. Benjamin DARST and Sally Payne. Sur. William Price. p 76

14 November 1785. James DAVENPORT and Dicey Kennaday,
dau. of Mary Kennedy. Sur. George Lunsden. Wit. Nancy
Kennedy and Robert Kennedy. Married 19 November by Rev.
John Waller. p 30

21 September 1779. Abraham DAVIS and Ann Johnson. Sur.
Archelaus Harris. Wit. Fanney Harris. Married 23
September by Rev. William Douglas who says Davies. p 13

25 July 1795. Alexander DAVIS and Judah Reynolds, dau.
of Philip Reynolds who is surety. Wit. Philip Reynolds,
Jr. and Joseph Reynolds. p 72

28 December 1804. Benjamin DAVIS and Frances HUMPHREY,
over 21 years of age, dau. of Edmond Humphrey. Sur.
John Moore. Wit. Jessup Humphrey. Married 29 December by Rev. William Baskett. p 114

24 December 1796. Charles DAVIS and Susanna Ragland,
(Sukey), 21 years of age. Sur. John Bagby, Jr. Wit.
Sally Michie. p 79

24 December 1794. George DAVIS and Rebecca Hall, dau.
of Timothy Hall. Sur. John Sharp. Wit. Nancey Sharp.
Married 10 January 1795 by Rev. Martin Walton. p 70

9 January 1815. Hartwell DAVIS and Alice Bunch. Sur.
Hartwell Davis. p 157

13 October 1800. James DAVIS and Salley Ragland.
Sur. Nathaniel Ragland. Wit. John Poindexter, Jr.
Married by Rev. John Lasley. p 95

11 February 1806. John DAVIS and Elizabeth Johnson.
Sur. Sanford R. Connelly. Wit. John Lasley. Married
by Rev. John Lasley. p 120

11 March 1811. John DAVIS and Mary Ragland. Sur.
Nathaniel Ragland. Married by Rev. John Lasley. p 143

14 August 1769. Samuel DAVIS and Annes Lipscomb. Sur.
James Barnett. p 2

13 August 1798. Thomas DAVIS and Elizabeth Gunnell.
Sur. John Gunnell. Married 30 August by Rev. William
Cooke who says Thomas T. Davis. p 85

25 November 1809. Thomas T. DAVIS and Matilda Fleming,
over 21 years of age. Sur. William Smith. p 137

12 April 1813. Tinsley DAVIS and Frances Ragland. Sur.
Nathaniel Ragland. Married 15 April by Rev. John
Lasley. p 152

12 September 1774. William DAVIS and Mary Gosney. Sur. James Barnett. p 8

30 March 1813. John DAY and Ann Talley. Sur. Joel Watkins. Wit. William Williams. Married by Rev. William Y. Hiter. Return dated ___ __.__ 1814. p 157

~~10 October 1795. Jacob DEALS and Frankey Harger, dau. of~~ John Harger. Sur. John Sharp. Wit. George Davis. Married 22 October by Rev. Martin Walton. p 73

3 November 1786. Jesse DEARVIN and Ann Watkins. Benjamin Watkins gives consent for Ann. Sur. John Ward. Wit. Thomas Gardner. p 33

24 October 1814. William DEDMAN and Betsy Bagby. Sur. John Beadles. Wit. George Thomasson. Married by Rev. William Y. Hiter. p 156

1 May 1797. Isham DESPER and Polley Henson. Sur. Robert Bell. Wit. Bartlett Henson. Married 3 May by Rev. William Baskett. p 81

2 March 1808. John DESPER and Margaret Porter (Magland Porter). Sur. Thomas Porter. Married 4 March by Rev. William Baskett who says Maglan. p 128

25 December 1810. Overton DESPER and Mary Fulcher. Sur. Allen Fulcher. Wit. John Fulcher. p 142

8 February 1790. Charles DICKASON and Nancey Sandidge. Sur. Richard Sandidge. Married by Rev. H. Goodloe who says Dickerson. Return dated 29 August 1790. p 49

20 October 1780. Richard DICKENS and Elizabeth Sansom. Married by Rev. William Douglas. The Douglas Register p 20

25 February 1783. John DICKIN and Catharine Dorrell Sansum. Sur. Nicholas Gentry. Wit. William Winslow. Married 6 March by Rev. William Douglas. p 22

24 January 1809. William DICKENSON and Ann P. Madison, over 21 years of age, dau. of Ambrose Madison. Each gives own consent. Sur. P. B. Madison. Married 26 January by Rev. William Cooke who says Dickinson. p 133

13 December 1813. Thomas DICKERSON and Maria Mallory. Sur. Henry Mallory. p 154

30 November 1782. Elijah DICKINSON and Susannah Smith. Sur. Richard Paulett. Married 3 December by Rev. William Douglas who says Dickerson. p 21

1 January 1798. Garland DICKINSON and Betsey Snelson, dau. of Nathaniel Snelson. Sur. Charles Fortson. Wit. Dabney Dickinson. p 83

6 September 1804. George DICKINSON and Patty Young, 'alias Meade', dau. of Henry Meade. Sur. Charles Cosby. Wit. John Payne. Married by Rev. Richard Ferguson. p 112

26 December 1796. Higgason Cosby DICKINSON and Nancy Graven, dau. of Thomas Graven. Sur. John Graven. Wit. John Foster and William Graven. Married 27 December by Rev. William Cooke who says Higgason C. Dickason. p 79

21 March 1795. James DICKINSON, Jr. and Susannah R. Dickinson, dau. of James Dickinson, Sr. Sur. Patrick Barkley. Wit. Hezekiah Dickinson and Charles Dickinson. p 71

14 October 1800. James C. DICKINSON and Marry Sandidge, dau. of Joseph Sandidge. Sur. John Boxley. Wit. Elizabeth Sandidge and George Boxley. James Dispins consents for James Cole Dickinson who is under age. Married by Rev. Richard Ferguson who says Mary. Return dated 19 August 1801. p 95

18 December 1798. Joel DICKINSON and Nancey Chewning, dau. of Jane Chewning. Sur. Jesse Chewning. Wit. Gene Chewning. (Eugene?) p 86

12 March 1810. John J. DICKINSON and Charlotte Harris, dau. of Nelson Harris. Sur. John Shelton, Jr. Wit. Bickerton Winston and Martha Harris. p 139

18 August 1806. Richard DICKINSON and Martha Crawford. Sur. Peter Crawford. Married 21 August by Rev. John Lasley. p 121

12 August 1796. William DICKINSON and Sarah Crenshaw. Sur. David Smith. Wit. Elizabeth Crenshaw and Saley Trice. Married 13 August by Rev. William Cooke who says Dickason. p 77

23 December 1805. William DICKINSON and Jane Crawford. John Crawford gives consent for Jane. Sur. Archibald Hutchinson. Wit. John Crawford, Jr. Married by Rev. John Lasley. p 119

27 November 1809. Dudley DIGGS and Judith Neale Maury, under 21 years of age, dau. of Benjamin Maury. Sur. Fontaine Maury. p 137

8 March 1790. John DIGGS and Dorothea Anthony. Sur.
James Anthony. p 49

3 February 1813. John DIGGS, Jr. and Elizabeth P.
Anthony, (Betsy). Sur. Nathaniel Anthony, Jr. Wit.
Lewis Anthony, James Higgason and N. B. Barrett. p 151

6 February 1809. Thomas DIGGS and Elizabeth Desper,
over 21 years of age, dau. of Thomas Desper. Josiah
Bunch makes affadavit Thomas is 21 years of age. Sur.
Moses Desper, Wit. Robert Watkins. Married by Rev.
William Baskett. p 134

17 June 1795. Joseph DOBLE and Barbara Estes. Sur.
Abraham Estes. Married by Rev. Richard Pope who says
Double. p 72

29 December 1803. John DOLTON, Junr and Patsy Bibb.
Sur. Zacheus Bailey. Married by Rev. John Lasley.
p 110

29 December 1804. Robert DOLTON and Sucky Hughes.
Married by Rev. John Lasley. Ministers' Returns p 378

29 February 1804. William DOLTON and Salley Wood. Sur.
Thomas Wood. Married 1 March by Rev. John Lasley. p 111

1 October 1796. James DOLS and Elizabeth Homes, dau. of
Duncan Homes. Sur. James Kennedy. Wit. William Wash.
p 77

15 January 1772. Robert DOUGLASS and Martha Bigger.
Sur. William Hughes. p 5

18 September 1815. Edward DOWNING and Elizabeth W.
Michie, dau. of William Michie. Sur. Fontaine Michie
or James F. Michie. Wit. Charles Downing. Edward son
of John Downing. p 159

10 June 1793. John DOWNING and Mary Michie. Sur.
William Michie. p 62

12 November 1798. Joseph DRAKE and Jane Lea. Sur.
John Lea. Married 13 November by Rev. William Baskett.
p 86

21 December 1808. David DRAPER and Frances Stephens.
Sur. James Rowe. Married by Rev. John B. Magruder of
the Methodist Episcopal Church. Returned 21 March
1809. p 132

8 December 1795. John DRAPER and Elizabeth Gooch.
Sur. Thomas Gooch. p 74

3 December 1804. John DRAPER and Polly Rowe, under 21 years of age, dau. of Jesse Rowe and niece of James Rowe who is surety. Wit. John Rowe and Jesse Rowe, Jr. Married 6 December by Rev. John Lasley. p 113

12 March 1812. John DRAPER, Jr. and Margaret Burrus, (Peggy), dau. of Roger Burrus. Sur. Nathaniel Mills, Jr. p 147

12 September 1788. Edward DUDLEY and Roxanna Smith. Sur. Robert Kimbrough. Married 17 September by Rev. William Douglas who says Rosanna. p 41

13 October 1778. Clevears DUKE and Elizabeth Barber Johnson. Sur. William Johnson. p 11

7 April 1783. Clevears DUKE and Mary Wash, dau. of William Wash. Sur. George Lumsden. Wit. John Wash, Jr. p 22

12 October 1770. Clevears DUKE and Lucy Smith. Sur. Dudley Brown and George Lumsden. p 3

12 April 1797. Cosby DUKE and Nancy Terry, dau. of Thomas Terry. Sur. Mills Terry. Married 15 April by Rev. William Baskett. p 81

17 November 1794. Edmund DUKE and Mary Dickinson. Sur. Thomas Dickinson. p 69

8 January 1812. Garland DUKE and Frances Gibson, dau. of William Gibson. Sur. Edmund Bullock. Wit. John Smith, Jr. and Thomas Duke. Married 14 January by Rev. William Cooke. p 146

7 April 1783. Harden DUKE and Betsey Swift, 21 years of age, dau. of Richard Swift. Sur. George Lumsden. Wit. John Swift and John Burnley. Married 15 April by Rev. William Douglas. p 23

26 December 1806. James DUKE and Nancey Biggers, over 21 years of age. Sur. Pleasant Carpenter. Married 28 December by Rev. William E. Waller. p 124

1 December 1786. Robert DUNCAN and Susannah Lane. Sur. David Lane. p 34

6 February 1786. Martin DUNN and Molley Anderson Hughes. Sur. William Hughes. p 31

8 April 1793. Martin DUNN and Patsey Terry. Sur. David Terry. Married 11 April by Rev. John Lasley. p 61

14 October 1805. Leonard DUNNAVANT and Elizabeth Groom, dau. of William Groom, deceased. Leonard Dunnavant is her guardian. Sur. Joel Parish. p 116

19 November 1788. John DURRETT and Martha Bibb (Patsy), dau. of Mary Bibb. Sur. Henry Bibb. Wit. Joshua Hughes and Ann Terry. John is son of Joel Durrett. Married by Rev. William Douglas who says Durrell. p 42

1 June 1796. Benjamin DURST and Sally Payne. Married by Rev. Richard Pope. Ministers' Returns p 369

11 March 1801. James T. DUVAL and Judith Jennings, dau. of Thomas and Sarah Jennings. Sur. John Jennings. Wit. Dudley Ragland. James T. is son of James Duval. Married 12 March by Rev. Richard Pope. p 97

8 June 1780. Claiborne DUVALL and Elizabeth Pope, dau. of Nathaniel Pope. Sur. John Nelson. Wit. Robert Barrett, William Duval and Philip Duval. Claiborne is son of Samuel Duval. p 15

8 June 1772. William DUVALL and Anne Pope, under 21 years of age, dau. of Nathaniel Pope. Sur. John Walker. Wit. John Bullock and William Bullock, Jr. p 5

10 January 1779. Henry DYCHES and Delany Haly. Married by Rev. William Douglas. The Douglas Register p 18

8 November 1773. James DYCHES and Tabitha Haley. Married by Rev. William Douglas. The Douglas Register p 14

28 September 1778. William DYCHES and Sarah Haley. Married by Rev. William Douglas. The Douglas Register p 18

14 December 1787. Samuel DYER and Celia Bickley. Sur. Charles Yancey. Wit. Elizabeth Bickley and Tho. Anderson. p 37

26 April 1782. George EARNEST and Catharine White, dau. of Col. William White. Sur. William White. Married 17 May by Rev. William Douglas who says George is of Hanover County. p 20

8 November 1796. William EDDES and Nancy Mann. Sur. Henry M. Groom. Wit. Thomas Mann, Jr. William is son of Thomas Eddes. p 78

15 March 1774. Ambrose EDWARDS and Olive Martin. Married by Rev. William Douglas. The Douglas Register p 15

14 December 1789. Ambrose EDWARDS and Dorothea Cannaday.
Sur. William Kennedy. Married 7 January 1790 by Rev.
Thomas Weatherford who says Dorothy Kennedy. p 48

15 November 1808. Daniel EDWARDS and Uny Gooch. Sur.
Rowland Gooch. p 131

22 July 1784. George EDWARDS and Francis Dickerson.
Married by Rev. William Douglas. The Douglas Register
p 23

11 May 1791. Gravit EDWARDS and Elizabeth Harris. Sur.
William Pettit. Married by Rev. William Douglas. p 54

17 December 1804. Henry EDWARDS and Nancey Lane. Sur.
Wright EdwaRds. Married by Rev. Richard Ferguson who
says Elizabeth. No date of marriage given. p 113

13 May 1805. Ivy EDWARDS and Pheby Gardner. Sur.
Thomas Gardner. p 116

9 January 1797. John EDWARDS and Nancy McGehee. Sur.
John McGehee. p 80

27 December 1782. Solomon EDWARDS and Sarah Mathews.
Married by Rev. William Douglas. The Douglas
Register p 22

1 January 1780. William EDWARDS and Anne Walton. Sur.
Rebecca Edwards. p 14

15 January 1805. Wright EDWARDS and Nancy Brown, under 21 years of age, dau. of Thomas Brown who is
surety. Wit. John W. Sale and Micajah Clarke. Married by Rev. Richard Ferguson. No date given. p 114

12 May 1785. Joseph EGGLESTON and Mary Duke. Sur.
Thomas Wash, Sr. p 28

8 October 1795. Michael EMRA (?) and Sisley Johnson.
Married by Rev. John Lasley. Ministers' Returns
p 368

24 November 1790. William ENGLAND and Rhoda Bunch, dau.
of Pouncey Bunch. Sur. Nathaniel Bunch. Wit. Thomas
Bunch. Married 25 November by Rev. John Lasley. p 52

13 February 1787. Abraham ESTIS and Sarah Timberlake.
Sur. Philip Timberlake. Married 14 February by Rev.
William Douglas. p 34

10 February 1800. Hasting EVANS and Lucy Willington, dau. of Thomas Willington. Sur. Lewis Johnson. Wit. James Hendrick and Caty Whittington. Married by Rev. Richard Ferguson. Return dated 11 August 1801. p 92

10 September 1810. John EVANS and Roseanna Johnson. Sur. David Dalton. Married 11 September by Rev. John Lasley. p 140

2 September 1794. Shelton EVANS and Mary Grinstead. John Grinstead gives consent for Mary. Sur. Emmanuel Evans. Wit. John Poindexter. p 68

19 October 1810. Jacob FACKLER and Carolina Matilda Morris, under 21 years of age, dau. of David Morris. Sur. George Morris, Jr. Jacob is of Staunton, Virginia. p 141

24 November 1782. William FARIS and Sally Johnston. Married by Rev. William Douglas who says Faries and Johnson. The Douglas Register p 22

14 November 1779. Edward FAR and Mary Perkins. Married by Rev. William Douglas. The Douglas Register p 19

6 November 1781. Abraham FARGUSON and Nancy Smith. Sur. William Smith. Married 8 November by Rev. William Douglas, p 18

23 November 1798. Richard FARGUSON and Elizabeth Douglass. Sur. James Beadles. Wit. Benjamin King. p 86

3 December 1804. Charles FARIS and Mildred Boyd, dau. of John Boyd. Sur. William Boyd. (See James Faris). p 113

6 December 1804. James FARIS and Mildred Boyd. Married by Rev. John Lasley. (See Charles Faris). Ministers' Returns p 380

16 September 1794. John FARIS and Mary Rowe, dau. of John Rowe, Sr. who is surety. Wit. Ste. Rowe. (Stephen ?) p 68

20 February 1809. Major John FARRAR and Salley Grubbs, dau. of Matthew Grubbs. Sur. William Grubbs. Wit. Martha Grubbs. p 134

2 May 1769. Richard FARRAR and Susanna Shelton, dau. of William Shelton who is surety. p 2

16 December 1806. William FARRAR and Elizabeth Barnett,
dau. of Robert F. Barnett who is surety. Married 17
December by Rev. William Baskett. p 123

15 November 1813. Benjamin FARRIS and Martha Bunch.
Sur. William Walker. Wit. George C. Wheeler. Married
16 November by Rev. John Lasley. p 154

24 November 1798. Richard FERGASON and Elizabeth Douglas.
Married by Rev. John Lasley. Ministers' Returns p 370

23 November 1779. Francis FIDLER and Sarah Stringer.
Sur. William White, Senr. p 13

13 August 1811. John D. FIELDING and Elizabeth Fielding. Eppa Fielding is her guardian. Sur. Ludlow
Bramham. p 144

10 April 1806. Ambrose FLANAGAN and Diannah Chewning,
over 21 years of age. Sur. Micajah Johnson. p 121

2 February 1803. Charles FLANAGAN and Elizabeth
Saunders, dau. of David Saunders. Sur. Julius Saun-
ders. Wit. George Saunders. (Also written Elizabeth
Sanders on the bond). p 105

9 December 1783. John FLEEMAN and Lovinah Gooch.
Sur. Rowland Gooch. p 24

26 December 1791. William Steel FLEEMAN and Elizabeth
Warren. Sur. Bartholomew Warren. Married 27 December
by Rev. John Waller. p 57

16 December 1795. Anthony FLEMING and Frances Harper,
of lawful age. Sur. Richard Luck. Wit. George
Lumsden. Married 24 December by Rev. William Cooke.
p 74

27 April 1815. Garland FLEMING and Maria Fleming.
Sur. John Fleming. Married 3 May by Rev. William
Cooke. p 158

10 December 1783. John FLEMING and Lovinah Clements.
Married by Rev. William Douglas. The Douglas Register
p 23

20 April 1786. John FLEMING and Elizabeth Harris,
dau. of Micajah Harris. Sur. Solomon Edwards. Wit.
John Kimbrough and Samuel Harris. p 32

4 August 1813. Robert FLEMING and Dorothy Davis. Sur.
John Fleming. Wit. Anthony Fleming and John Luck.
Married 5 August by Rev. William Cooke. p 152

89

17 October 1796. William FLEMING and Susanna Davis
(Sukey), upwards of 21 years of age, dau. of Anna Davis.
Sur. John Fleming. Wit. William Spicer. Married 20
October by Rev. John Waller. p 47

22 December 1794. Abraham FLETCHER and Catharine Timberlake, dau. of Philip Timberlake. Sur. Abraham Estes.
Wit. Sary Estes. p 70

2 May 1793. Gideon FLOYD and Sally Morris. Sur. David
Morris. p 62

10 May 1773. Aaron FONTAINE and Barbara Terrell. Major
Zachary Lewis is her guardian. Sur. Samuel Temple.
Wit. John Overton, Fras. Bickley, Richard Dabney and
Owen Gwathmey, Jr, p 6

2 November 1774. Francis FORD and Mary Gardner. Sur.
John Gardner, p 9

20 January 1808. William FORD and Polly Allen. Sur.
Peter Butler. Wit. David Allen. Married 11 February
by Rev. William Cooke. p 128

16 October 1788. Charles FORSAN and Molly Luck. Married by Rev. John Waller. Ministers' Returns p 362

2 October 1768. James FORSYTH and Elizabeth Jones.
Sur. Edward Jones, p 1

12 August 1800. William FORTSON and Rebecca Cole, over
21 years of age. Sur. Armistead Cole. Married by Rev.
Richard Ferguson. Returned 19 August 1801. p 94

30 January 1805. Chisholm FORTUNE and Barbara Gibson,
dau. of Thornton Gibson. Sur. Thomas Smith. Married
31 January by Rev. William Cooke. p 115

19 December 1787. Bartlett FOSTER and Elizabeth Harris,
dau. of Micajah Harris who is surety. Wit. John Timberlake and Gideon Mitchell. Bartlett is son of James
Foster of Fluvanna County. Married 23 December by Rev.
John Lasley. p 38

13 October 1788. Charles FOSTER and Molly Luck, of age.
Sur. Benjamin Hancock. Wit. Elizabeth Dickinson and
Larkin Luck. p 42

10 December 1798. Francis FOSTER and Polley Shepard.
Robert Shepard gives consent for Polley. Sur. John
Foster. Wit. John Perdexter. (Poindexter?) p 86

15 December 1788. John FOSTER and Molly Harris.
Nathaniel Harris makes affadavit as to Molly's age and
is surety. John is upwards of 21 years of age. p 43

9 February 1789. John FOSTER and Agnes Ward, dau. of
William Ward. Sur. John Ward. Wit. William Armstrong
and Thomas Gardner. p 44

7 March 1815. John FOSTER, Jr. and Theodshe Christmas.
Sur. David Armstrong. John is son of John Foster, Sr.
p 157

10 March 1794. Lanslott FOSTER and Sarah Ryan, dau.
of William Ryan. Sur. William Griffin. Wit. John
Foster. Married 18 March by Rev. Martin Walton, who
says Larencelott. p 66

23 March 1791. Nelson FOSTER and Elizabeth Thomasson,
dau. of William Thomasson. Sur. John Hubbard. Wit.
Carter Hubbard. Married 24 March by Rev. John Lasley.
p 53

12 November 1795. Nelson FOSTER and Nancey Harris,
dau. of Elizabeth Edwards. Sur. Stephen Terry. p 73

11 December 1812. Richard FOSTER and Dicey Thacker.
Sur. John Normant. Richard, 23 years of age, is son
of Mary Foster. Married 18 December by Rev.
Claibourn Walton. p 150

9 March 1789. William FOSTER and Elizabeth Lovell,
dau. of William Lovell. Sur. Peter Shelton. Wit.
John Lovell and George Lovell. p 44

2 July 1803. John FRANK and Catharine Smith. Sur.
Drury Jones. Married by Rev. John Lasley. p 106

1 June 1782. Alexander FRAZIER and Judith Hill, dau.
of James Hill. Sur. Robert Freeman. Wit. Asa Hall
and Richard Johnson. p 20

22 December 1808. George FREEMAN and Elizabeth
Dickinson. Thomas and Sarah Dickerson give
consent for Elizabeth. Sur. Thomas Dickerson.
Wit. William Perry. p 132

8 March 1802. Josiah FREEMAN and _ _ _ _ _ _ _ _ .
Sur. Dabney Freeman. Married by Rev. Richard
Ferguson who says Elizabeth _ _ _ _ _ _ . Returned
with a group of marriages 1 May 1804. p 101

14 August 1815. Robert FREEMAN and Mary Parrish. Sur.
Parks Parrish. Married 16 August by Rev. Claibourn
Walton. p 159

28 May 1795. Zachariah FREEMAN and Patsey Rice, dau. of
Sary Rice. Sur. William Hunter. Wit. Stephen Farrar.
Married 31 May by Rev. Hugh French. p 71

6 April 1776. Simon FRENSLY and Elizabeth Walden. Sur.
Charles Walden. p 10

18 April 1787. Thomas FRETWELL and Agnes Crenshaw, dau.
of William A. Crenshaw. Sur. David Crenshaw. Wit. John
Burley and Charles Cosby. p 35

18 December 1789. William FRETWELL and Jemima Crenshaw.
Sur. David Crenshaw. p 48

22 April 1809. Jesse FULCHER and Patsy Seargeant, Jun[r].,
dau. of Patsy Seargeant. Sur. Harrison Seargeant.
Married 24 April by Rev. John Lasley. p 135

11 November 1789. Bartholomew FULLER and Christian Allen.
Sur. James Allen. Wit. William Pollock, Jr. p 47

22 December 1794. John GAFFNEY and Blendina Bowen, dau.
of Anne Bowen. Sur. John Mickie. Wit. G. Cary. p 70

20 January 1806. John GALBRAITH and Caty Peers, dau.
of Thomas Peers, Sr. Sur. Micajah Sims. Married by
Rev. Richard Ferguson. p 119

26 December 1789. William GAMON and Temperance Gardner,
dau. of John Gardner. Sur. Daniel Gardner. Wit. Thomas
Gardner and George Fletcher. Married by Rev. William
Douglas who says Gammon. p 48

15 December 1792. Daniel GARDNER and Mercy Anthony.
James Anthony gives consent for Mercy. Sur. John Diggs.
Wit. John Fretwell. p 60

14 April 1800. William GARDNER and Catharine Hollins.
Sur. Benjamin Hollins. Married by Rev. Richard Ferguson. The return is dated 19 August 1801. p 93

15 May 1800. Edward GARLAND and Elizabeth Morris, dau.
of Richard Morris. Sur. Richard Morris, Jr. p 93

9 February 1795. Robert GARLAND, Jun[r]. and Elizabeth
Bullock. Sur. Robert Bullock. p 71

15 October 1790. John GARLAND and Lucy Gordon. Sur. Jonathan Gordon. Married by Rev. William Douglas. p 51

22 December 1809. Major T. GARNETT and Fanny Sledd, under 21 years of age, dau. of John Sledd. Sur. Thomas Sledd. p 138

16 February 1796. Henry GARRETT and Patsey Anderson, dau. of Amediah Anderson. Sur. William G. Johnson. Wit. Sally M. anderson and Ann Lee. Married 17 February by Rev. William Cooke. p 75

14 February 1803. Henry GARRETT and Judith Peers. Sur. Thomas Peers. p 105

8 December 1794. William GARRETT and Elizabeth Y.Smith. Sur. Nathaniel Ragland. Married 12 December by Rev. Martin Walton. p 69

7 December 1770. William GARRETT, Jr. and Ann Johnson. Sur. Henry Garrett. p 3

14 March 1786. Blaxton GENTRY and Mary Bunch, dau. of James Bunch. Sur. John Bunch. Wit. William Bunch. p 31

15 January 1778. James GENTRY and Sarah Dickerson. Sur. William Poindexter. p 10

1 April 1780. John GENTRY and Milly Edwards. Sur. Grant Edwards. p 14

4 January 1799. John GENTRY and Barbara Hogard, dau. of Jesse Hogard. Sur. William Plant. Wit. William G. Poindexter, Thomas Wash and Benjamin Duke. Married 5 January by Rev. Martin Walton who says Hoggard. p 87

1 January 1814. Nicholas GENTRY and Nancy Carrel, of age. Sur. Lewis Padgett. Married by Rev. Claibourne Walton. p 154

23 October 1802. Patrick GENTRY and Mary Ann Porter. Each party is over 21 years of age. Sur. William Whitlock, Jr. p 102

19 April 1796. Richard GENTRY and Rebecca Barnett, dau. of William Barnett. Sur. Nathaniel Harris. Wit. Allen Foster and Judith Foster. Married by Rev. John Lasley. p 76

6 December 1809. Robert GENTRY and Elizabeth Kersey. John Thomasson is guardian of Elizabeth. Robert is over 21 years of age. Sur. Stephen Harris. p 137

31 May 1813. Robert GENTRY and Mary Marks, 21 years of age. Sur. William Sledd. p 152

24 April 1787. William GENTRY and Elizabeth Kersey, dau. of Thomas Kersey. Sur. Story Talley. Wit. Thomas Gardner, Daniel Gardner and Exex^r. Kersey. p 35

24 June 1808. Wyatt GENTRY and Polly Amos. Sur. Hezekiah Dunnavant. Married 30 June. The Minister's name is not given. p 129

20 October 1784. Robert GEORGE and Susanna Burton. Sur. Charles Burton. p 27

3 September 1814. Dudley A. GIBSON and Jane Armstrong. Sur. John Armstrong, Jr. p 155

15 October 1792. Gilbert GIBSON and Mildred Lowry. Sur. William Bradbury. p 59

8 January 1779. James GIBSON and Sally Tally. Married by Rev. William Douglas. The Douglas Register p 18

11 July 1791. James Dabney GIBSON and Nancey Talley. Sur. David Trainum. p 55

13 March 1783. John GIBSON and Mary Tally. Married by Rev. William Douglas. The Douglas Register p 22

20 May 1815. Johnson GIBSON and Lucy Gibson. Sur. Nathan Gibson. Married 23 May by Rev. Claibourne Walton. p 158

10 May 1791. Lightfoot GIBSON and Frances Davis. Sur. William Gibson. p 54

28 November 1815. Nathan GIBSON and Lucy Shepherd, dau. of Philip Shepherd. Sur. Jeremiah Sprouse. p 160

29 November 1815. Oswald GIBSON and Maria A. Dickenson, dau. of H. C. Dickenson. Sur. William Anderson. Wit. Thomas Baker, John B. Dickinson and Anne Dickinson. p 159

25 November 1788. William GIBSON and Mary Terry, dau. of Henriter Terry. Sur. William Nuckols. p 42

29 December 1808. Zedekiah GIBSON and Nancey Mallory, (Ann), over 21 years of age. Sur. John Gentry. Wit. Jesse Hogard and Nath. Snelson. p 133

1 October 1782. Francis GIDDENS and Mary White. Sur. Moses White. Married 3 October by Rev. William Douglas who says Giddin. p 21

13 November 1780. William GIDDENS and Susanna Wood.
Sur. William Wood. (See William Giddin). p 15

16 November 1780. William GIDDIN and Susanna West.
Married by Rev. William Douglas. (See William Giddens.)
The Douglas Register p 20

10 January 1807. John GILBERT, Jr. and Mary Haines.
Sur. John Bibb. Married 14 January by Rev. William
Baskett. p 124

10 December 1813. Reubin GILBERT and Jane Jones. Sur.
Thomas Jones. Married 17 December by Rev. John Lasley.
p 154

16 August 1810. Samuel GILBERT and Cassandra Campbell.
F. L. Campbell gives consent for Cassandra. Sur. __ __
__ __ __ ? Wit. Hopeful Toler. p 140

20 January 1791. David GILLASPY and Frances Robards.
Sur. Maurice Robards. p 53

28 September 1801. David GILLASPY and Margaret Saunders.
Julius Saunders, her brother, makes affadavit that Margaret is over 21 years of age and is surety. p 99

26 December 1785. George GILLASBY and Molly Faris.
Sur. Charles Faris. p 30

16 December 1791. James GILLIAM and Susanna Smith, dau.
of Nathan Smith. Sur. William Gilliam. Married 22 __ __
(17)91 by Rev. William Douglas. p 57

14 December 1790. William GILLIAM and Elizabeth Barclay.
Sur. James Dickinson. Married 23 December by Rev. John
Waller. p 52

23 January 1810. Jackey GILLUM and Patsey Groom, over
21 years of age. Sur. John Bradley. Wit. Amos Gillum
and John Collins. Jackey is son of William Gillum.
Married by Rev. John Lasley. p 139

7 December 1802. John GILLUM and Betsey Smith, dau. of
George Smith. Sur. Barnett Smith. Wit. John Smith.
p 103

16 February 1803. Archer GLASS and Susanna Thompson,
dau. of Elizabeth Thompson. Sur. John Thompson. Wit.
R. Henley. Married by Rev. Richard Pope. p 105

13 December 1802. Martin GLASS and Lucy M. Amos, dau.
of Sarah Amos. Sur. John Johnson. Married by Rev.
Richard Pope. p 104

8 October 1811. Charles GLENN and Nancey Fleming, under age, dau. of John Fleming who is surety. Married 10 October by Rev. William Cooke. p 145

24 July 1784. John GLENN and Mary Bolton. Sur. Charles Thomas. Wit. Benjamin Stark and John Poindexter, Jr. p 26

7 October 1789. John GLENN and Mildret Trainom, dau. of Charles Trainom. Sur. David Trainum. Wit. John Tretwell (Fretwell?) and Mourning Tretwell. p 46

21 December 1793. John GLENN, Jr. and Polley Brooks. Sur. Richeson Brooks. Married 23 December by Rev. Richard Pope. p 65

13 October 1803. Simeon GLENN and Nancey Moss. William Johnson is guardian of Nancey. Sur. Thomas Glenn. Wit. Sarah Johnson. Married 20 October by Rev. Lewis Chaudoin. p 108

12 March 1783. Claiborne GOOCH and Mildred Thomson. Sur. Rowland Gooch. Married 13 March by Rev. William Douglas. p 22

11 June 1804. Dabney GOOCH and Ruth Dunn. Sur. Liner Gooch and Martin Dunn. p 112

12 February 1790. Gideon GOOCH and Rosa Settle. Sur. Claibourne Gooch. p 49

3 November 1794. Gideon GOOCH and Sally Maddison, dau. of John Maddison. Sur. Benjamin Hollins. p 69

11 October 1803. James GOOCH and Elizabeth Anthony. James and Mary Anthony give consent for Elizabeth. Sur. James G. Sharp. Wit. Daniel Gardner. Married by Rev. Richard Ferguson. Returned with a group of marriages 1 May 1804. p 108

28 April 1780. Linor GOOCH and Rhoda Turner, dau. of William Turner. Sur. Rowland Gooch. Wit. John Gooch. Linor is also written Aliney on the bond. Married by Rev. William Douglas. p 14

24 June 1809. Overton GOOCH and Polley C. Cole, over 21 years of age. Sur. Thomas Brown. Wit. John Cole. p 136

13 April 1801. Rowland GOOCH and Betsey McGehee. Sur. Duke W. Hallum. Wit. Mallson McGehee. Married 16 April by Rev. Duke W. Hullum. p 98

26 September 1808. Stephen GOOCH and Catharine Dickinson,
Robert Dickason gives consent for Catharine. Sur. Joel
Dickinson. Married 27 September by Rev. William Cooke.
p 130

14 January 1799. Thomas GOOCH and Patsy Tisdale. Sur.
John Tisdale. p 87

24 December 1808. Thompson GOOCH and Patsy Wood. Sur.
Thomas Wood. Thompson is also written Thomson on the
bond. Married 26 December by Rev. John Lasley. p 133

26 December 1783. Umphrey GOOCH and Mary Wagstaff.
Married by Rev. William Douglas. The Douglas Register
p 23

29 October 1802. William GOOCH and Elizabeth Terry.
Sur. Gideon Gooch. Wit. George Morris. p 103

24 March 1813. William D. GOOCH and Matilda Chiles.
Sur. John Chiles. p 151

7 January 1788. George GOODLOE and Judith Holland, dau.
of George Holland. Sur. Michael Holland. Wit. Phil
Goodloe and Salley Holland. Married 10 January by Rev.
H. Goodloe. p 38

22 December 1806. William GOODMAN, Jr. and Jane Clough,
dau. of Richard Clough who is surety. p 123

13 September 1805. Archibald GOODWIN and Candace Sandidge,
dau. of Joseph Sandidge. Sur. James C. Dickinson. Wit.
Mary Dickerson and Robert Goodwin. Jane Goodwin is
guardian of Archibald. Married by Rev. Richard Ferguson. p 116

12 April 1810. Edmund C. GOODWIN and Elizabeth Waddy,
over 21 years of age. Sur. Richard Anderson. p 139

26 December 1803. John GOODWIN and Anne Thomson, dau.
of William Thomson. Sur. Hugh Goodwin. Wit. Mary Duke
and William Thomson, Jr. Married 27 December by Rev.
A. Waller who says Thompson. p 109

14 June 1813. John GOODWIN and Elizabeth Napper. Sur.
Jeremiah Sprouce. Wit. Nelson B. Barret. p 152

9 December 1766. Robert GOODWIN and Jane Tolloh. Sur.
Clevers Duke. p 1

10 November 1814. William D. GOODWIN and Mary W. Cosby.
Sur. Benjamin H. Cosby. p 156

20 November 1787. Mark H. GOOLESBERY and Jane Duke, dau. of Henry Duke. Sur. Cosby Fosler. (Foster?) Wit. Thomas Gardner. p 37

4 January 1775. George GORDON and Sarah Herndon. Sur. Joseph Holladay, Jr. p 9

28 May 1796. Jonathan GORDON and Elander Garland. Sur. John Lane. Wit. Eliza Garland. p 76

9 October 1797. Joseph GRADY and Catharine Bond Yancey, (Kitty), granddaughter of Thomas Bond. Sur. Wright Bond. Wit. Malcolm Hart. Married 19 October by Rev. William Cooke. p 82

8 October 1793. William GRADY and Mary Leonard. Sur. Lewis Syms or Sins. Wit. Waddy Thomson, Jr. Married by Rev. H. Goodloe. No date is given. p 63

28 April 1780. Alexander GRANT and Martha Parish. Sur. John Parker. p 15

15 August 1803. Anderson GRAVEN and Joice Houchins, dau. of Francis Houchings. Sur. John Houchins. Wit. Judith W. Smith. Married by Rev. Richard Ferguson. p 107

8 August 1795. John GRAVEN and Patsey R. Duke. Married by Rev. William Cooke. Ministers' Returns p 367

5 January 1803. William GRAVEN and Polly Spencer, over 21 years of age. Sur. Meredith Cosby. p 104

16 April 1787. Bartlet GRAVES and Frances Lane, dau. of Henry Lane who is surety. Wit. Laurence Young and Rice Graves. Married 18 April by Rev. William Douglas. p 35

17 November 1802. James GRAVES and Elizabeth Ashton Garrett. William Garrett gives consent for Elizabeth. Sur. Henry Garrett. p 103

20 December 1784. John GRAVES and Lydia Graves, dau. of Thomas Graves. Sur. William Graves. Wit. Samuel Graves and Bartlett Graves. p 27

24 August 1795. John GRAVES and Mary Ragland. Sur. Francis L. Campbell. Wit. Thomas Poindexter and Martha Ragland. p 72

23 October 1790. Joseph GRAVES and Mary Goodwin. Jane Goodwin gives consent for Mary. Sur. Hugh Goodwin. Wit. John Poindexter. Married 26 October by Rev. John Waller. p 51

20 November 1780. Richard GRAVES and Sally Arnett.
James Arnett gives consent for Sally. Sur. James
Arnett, Jr. Wit. William Graves. Married 23 November
by Rev. William Douglas. p 15

17 November 1783. Samuel GRAVES and Sarah Graves, dau.
of Thomas Graves. Sur. William Graves. Wit. William
Lea. Married 20 November. No Minister's name is
given. p 24

28 August 1806. Thomas GRAVES and Delphia Edds, dau.
of Thomas Edds. Sur. James Wash. Wit. William Davenport. Married by Rev. John Lasley. p 121

1 February 1778. William GRAVES and Ann Pettus, dau.
of William Pettus. Sur. John Arnold. Wit. George
Lumsden and John Lumsden. p 11

29 December 1779. William GRAVES and Judith Harrison.
John Harrison gives consent for Judith. Sur. Richard
Graves. Wit. Hiram Harrison. p 14

7 August 1795. John GRAVIN and Patsy Read Duke. Sur.
Thomas W. Cosby. Wit. Elizabeth Yancey. p 72

3 November 1795. Thomas GRAY and Kitty Young. Sur.
James Young. p 73

Near Christmas 1802. William GREAVEN and Polly Spencer.
Married by Rev. Elisha Purington. Ministers' Returns
p 379

28 January 1780. Forest GREEN and Martha Green. Married by Rev. William Douglas. The Douglas Register
p 19

22 July 1800. Thomas GREEN and Nancy Grantler. Married by Rev. John Lasley. Ministers' Returns p 374

16 July 1801. George GREENHOW and Elizabeth A. Lewis.
Sur. John S. Smith. p 98

9 July 1787. Christopher GREENUP and Caty Pope, dau.
of Nathaniel Pope. Sur. William Duval. Wit. Nathaniel
Pope, Jr. and Pircy Pope. (Percy?) p 36

23 December 1795. John GRESHAM and Lyddia Hill, dau.
of David Hill. Sur. Japheth Painter. Wit. William
Thomson. p 74

4 September 1793. David GRIMSTEAD and Ann Warren.
Sur. James Poindexter. p 63

22 December 1802. Jasper GRINSTEAD and Jemima Gooch.
Sur. John Fleeman. Married by Rev. Duke W. Hallam.
p 104

29 December 1795. John GRISSON and Lydda Hill. Married
by Rev. John Lasley. Ministers' Returns. p 368

19 January 1808. Charles GROOM and Betsey Whitlock.
Sur. Thomas Whitlock. p 128

1 May 1815. James GROOM and Elizabeth Hunter. Sur.
John Poindexter, Jr. Married 4 May by Rev. Claibourne
Walton. p 158

8 August 1803. John GROOM and Mary Nelson, (Polly).
Sur. William Cooke. Wit. Ann Cooke. Married 11
August by Rev. William Cooke. p 107

8 January 1798. Major GROOM and Christiana Bibb. Sur.
John Bibb. p 83

9 March 1795. Richard GROOM and Barbara McGehee, dau.
of John McGehee, Sr. Sur. Vadin Sims. p 71

28 March 1786. Robert GROOM and Frances Parrish. John
Maddison gives consent for each party and is surety.
Wit. John Poindexter, Jr. and James Trice. p 32

17 January 1788. Robert GROOM and Elizabeth Bibb. Sur.
Thomas Bibb. Wit. James Bibb and Richard Henderson.
Married 18 January by Rev. William Douglas. p 39

9 September 1811. William GROOM and Patsey Butler.
Sur. John Kennon, Senr. Married 12 September by Rev.
John Lasley. p 144

27 October 1783. Matthew GRUBBS and Salley Shelton,
dau. of William Shelton. Sur. Richard Johnson. Wit.
__? Johnson. Married 27 October by Rev. William
Douglas. p 23

7 November 1799. Thomas GRUBBS and Patsey Call Anderson, dau. of John and Sarah Anderson. Patsey resides
in the home of Thomas Johnson. Sur. John L. Walton.
Wit. Nelson Anderson, Mary Johnson and Sarah Anderson.
p 91

21 August 1807. John GUNNELL and Lucy Fleming, dau.of
John Fleming. Sur. Robert Yancey. Wit. W. Cooke.
Married 22 August by Rev. William Cooke. p 125

28 August 1809. Charles GUNTER and Elizabeth Ware.
Sur. Dudley Ware. p 136

1 August 1810. Enos GUNTER and Frances Carpenter, over
21 years of age. Sur. John Gunter. Married 2 August
by Rev. W. E. Waller. p 140

17 March 1806. James GUNTER and Susanna Sims. Sur.
Benjamin Sims. Married 18 March by Rev. John Lasley.
p 120

18 August 1804. John GUNTER and Polly Carpenter, over
age. Sur. William Carpenter. p 112

4 October 1799. Thomas GUNTER and Mary Ware, over 21
years of age, sister of Dudley Ware who is surety.
Thomas is son of John Gunter, Sr. Married 8 October
by Rev. Richard Ferguson. p 90

15 November 1808. Pleasant HACKETT and Lucy Ragland.
Sur. John Graves. Married by Rev. John Lasley. p 131

6 December 1790. John M. HADEN and Mary Hopkins, of
age. Sur. Whittle Flanagan. Wit. Samuel Harris and
William Haden. Married 7 December by Rev. John Lasley.
p 52

18 February 1779. Benjamin HALEY and Judith Dyches.
Married by Rev. William Douglas. The Douglas
Register p 18

1 November 1773. William HALEY and Elizabeth Clark.
Married by Rev. William Douglas. The Douglas
Register p 14

11 April 1796. Absalom HALL and Rachel Watkins, dau.
of Benjamin Watkins. Sur. Jesse Darwin. Wit. Thomas
Gardner. Married 12 May by Rev. Martin Walton. p 76

27 April 1807. Asborn HALL and Jane Wash, niece of
Joseph Eggleston who consents. Sur. Richard E. Eggles -
ton. Married 30 April by Rev. Samuel Luck who says
Ashburn. p 125

27 August 1796. David HALL and Sarah McGehee. Sur.
William Cooke. Wit. James Hall and John Harper.
Married by Rev. William Cooke. p 77

21 December 1808. George HALL and Mary Harper, under
age, dau. of John and Elizabeth Harper. Sur. James
Wash. Wit. James Wash, Jr. and William Harper. Married 5 January 1809 by Rev. William Cooke. p 132

6 December 1788. James HALL and Nancy Pettit, of age, dau. of William Pettit. Mrs. Henritter Terry makes affadavit as to Nancy's age. Sur. Richmond Harris. Wit. Frederick Harris and James Nuckolls. Married 11 December by Rev. Charles Hopkins. p 42

20 December 1809. James HALL and Huldah Graves, over 21 years of age. Sur. Charles Thompson, Jr. Wit. Edm. Banks. Married 22 December by Rev. William Cooke. p 138

11 January 1814. John HALL and Patsy Harper, dau. of John and Betsy Harper. Sur. George Hall. p 155

3 February 1813. Martin HALL and Mildred Grubbs, (Milly), dau. of Benjamin Grubbs. Sur. Reuben Sims. Married 4 February by Rev. William Cooke. p 157

11 October 1784. Nathan HALL and Mary Wood. Sur. William Wood. Married 12 October by Rev. William Douglas. p 26

5 October 1791. Simion HALL and Nancey Porter, dau. of William Porter, Sr. Sur. Thomas Porter. Wit. W. Porter, Jr. p 56

3 March 1794, Zedekiah HALL and Sarah Davies. Sur. Story Talley. Wit. Elizabeth Talley and Thomas Gardner. Married 6 March by Rev. Martin Walton who says Davis. p 66

15 March 1793. Zephaniah HALL and Catharine Armstrong. Sur. Launcelott Foster. Wit. Thomas Gardner. Married 17 March by Rev. Martin Walton. p 61

3 December 1794. Edward HALLAM and Mary Dabney, dau. of J. W. Dabney. Sur. Thomas Hardin. Wit. James Byars. p 69

26 October 1783. Benjamin HALLIDAY and Sally Hampton. Married by Rev. William Douglas. The Douglas Register p 23

17 March 1815. George HAM and Susan Reynolds. Sur. Pleasant Kent. p 157

25 February 1790. David HAMILTON and Elizabeth Poindexter, dau. of William Poindexter. Sur. Meredith Poindexter. Wit. Daniel Gardner. p 49

23 August 1813. John HANCOCK and Susan P. Graves. Sur. James Hall. Married 24 August by Rev. William Cooke who says Susanna. p 153

27 December 1781. Austin HANCOCKE and Ann Nichols.
Married by Rev. William Douglas. The Douglas Register
p 21

24 April 1809. Gideon HANES and Frances Linch, over 21
years of age. Sur. Pleasant Hanes. Wit. Christopher
Hanes. p 135

24 December 1797. John HANES and Mary Bibb. Married
by Rev. Richard Pope. Ministers' Returns p 369

3 January 1805. Peter HANES and Nancey Bibb, dau. of
Henry Bibb, deceased. Sur. John Bibb. Wit. Sarah
Bibb. Married by Rev. Richard Ferguson. No date is
given. p 114

9 June 1800. Robert HANES and Sarah Dickinson, (also
written Sarah Dickason on the bond). John Dickason
gives consent for Sarah. Sur. William Dickason. p 93

17 November 1787. Thomas HARDIN and Ann Anderson
Dabney. James Dabney gives consent for Ann. Sur.
Christopher Johnson. Wit. John Hicks. p 37

30 January 1773. Giles HARDINE and Amy Morris. Married by Rev. William Douglas. The Douglas Register
p 14

20 September 1781. Joel HARKINS and Barbara Harris.
Married by Rev. William Douglas. The Douglas
Register p 21

25 December 1806. Charles HARLOW and Mary Crews.
William and Mary Crews give consent for Mary. Sur.
Jesse Crews. Wit. Miles G. Bardin and Jesse Cruse.
Married 28 December by Rev. William Baskett. p 123

12 February 1806. Daniel HARNER and Polly Crask,
over 21 years of age. Sur. John Watson. p 120

1 January 1788. John HARPER and Elizabeth Sims.
William Sims is guardian of Elizabeth. Sur. James
Hall. Wit. Austin Yeamans and Ananias Hall. John
Harper was 22 years old 5 March 1787. p 38

25 November 1781. Joseph HARPER and Ann Murphy.
Married by Rev. William Douglas. The Douglas
Register p 21

19 December 1815. William HARPER and Elizabeth Sims,
over 21 years of age. Sur. John Hall. p 160

6 June 1815. Barnet D. HARRIS and Isabella Trice. Sur.
Dabney Trice. Married by Rev. William Y. Hiter. p 158

10 February 1794. Benjamin HARRIS and Sally Overstreet.
Sur. Richard Jones. p 66

6 January 1803. Benjamin HARRIS and Mariah Harris. Sur.
Robert Harris. p 104

14 March 1803. Charles HARRIS and Polley Lipscomb.
Sur. William G. Poindexter. p 106

8 May 1783. Cyrus HARRIS and Elizabeth Bond. Married
by Rev. William Douglas. The Douglas Register p 23

6 February 1807. Damon HARRIS and Sarah King, dau. of
Higgason King. Sur. John Gentry. Wit. Charles Brooks,
Anne Harris and Elizabeth Brooks. p 125

27 January 1790. Deamon HARRIS and Susanna Woolams.
Sur. John Woolams. p 49

10 December 1805. Frederick HARRIS and Catherine S.
Smith. Sur. William G. Poindexter. p 118

8 November 1803. George HARRIS and Mary H. Cooke, dau.
of William Cooke. Sur. Richard Harris. Wit. Edward N.
Cooke and Frances Cooke. Married 9 November by Rev.
William Cooke. p 108

15 October 1799. Graves HARRIS and Elizabeth Wheeler,
dau. of Mark Wheeler. Sur. Edward Massie. Married by
Rev. John Lasley. p 90

2 January 1788. James HARRIS and Margery Bunch, dau.
of James Bunch. Sur. Nathaniel Harris. Wit. James
Trice and Thomas Barnett. Married 4 January by Rev.
John Lasley. p 38

19 April 1801. Jesse HARRIS and Polley Boxley, dau.
of Catharine Boxley who is her guardian. Sur. Thomas
Boxley, Jr. Wit. Joseph Boxley. p 98

5 September 1785. Job: HARRIS and Mary Farmer. Married by Rev. William Douglas, The Douglas Register
p 24

14 July 1792. John HARRIS and Polly Walker, dau. of
Peter Walker. Sur. Jesse Harris. Wit. Moses Harris.
p 58

26 August 1793. John HARRIS and Elizabeth Winn, dau. of Ann Harris. Sur. David Hambleton. Wit. John Word. Married 29 August by Rev. Martin Walton. p 62

22 December 1797. John HARRIS and Mary Bibb. Sur. Henry Bibb. Wit. Robert Thomson. p 83

17 February 1813. John HARRIS and Lucy P. Mallory, dau. of John Mallory. Sur. David Stewart. p 151

3 January 1805. Joseph HARRIS and Nancy Nuckolls, dau. of Thomas Nuckolls. Sur. Austin Hancock. Wit. James D. Nuckolls. Married by Rev. William Cooke. p 114

25 February 1809. Lewis HARRIS and Lucy Martin. William Martin makes affadavit that Lucy is of age. Sur. David Gray. p 134

27 May 1788. Nathaniel HARRIS and Martha Byars. Sur. Fleming Thomasson. Married 29 May by Rev. William Douglas. p 40

9 November 1789. Nelson HARRIS and Mary Pryor, over 21 years of age. William Smith is Bondsman. p 47

15 October 1789. Overton HARRIS and Jemima Harris, dau. of Frederick Harris. Sur. Robert Harris, Jr. and Ann O. Harris. p 46

2 September 1808. Peter HARRIS and Elizabeth McAllister. Sur. David Armstrong. p 130

29 March 1800. Richard HARRIS and Rhoda Thomasson, dau. of Elias Thomasson. Sur. Overton Harris. Wit. E. N. Thomasson. p 93

9 December 1810. Richard HARRIS and Jane Nuckolls. Sur. Thomas Nuckolls. Married 10 December by Rev. William Cooke. p 142

12 September 1791. Richmond HARRIS and Hendley Bickley, dau. of John Bickley. Sur. John Toler. Wit. John Yancey. p 56

20 July 1784. Robert HARRIS and Mary Davis, widow. Thomas Anderson was appointed guardian of Mary in Hanover County. Sur. Elias Thomason. Wit. Edward Harris. Married 22 July by Rev. William Douglas. p 25

13 February 1804. Robert HARRIS, Jr. and Elizabeth Baker, dau. of William Baker, Sr. Sur. Stephen Crank. Wit. Samuel Baker, Jr. Married by Rev. Richard Ferguson. Returned 1 May 1804. p 111

15 April 1809. Robert HARRIS and Elizabeth Burnley, dau. of James Burnley. Sur. William Jarman, Jr. Wit. H. W. Burnley and Jarrot Harris. p 135

29 October 1794. Samuel HARRIS and Rhoda Davis. Henry Davis gives consent for Rhoda and Robert Harris, Jr. consents for Samuel. Sur. Charles Bunch. Wit. George Poindexter. p 68

27 November 1809. Samuel HARRIS and Lydia Cole. Sur. John Cole. Wit. Richard Tyler and Samuel Cole. p 137

2 February 1807. Stephen HARRIS and Nancey Kersey. John Thomason is Nancy's guardian. Sur. Matthew Plant. Wit. Edward Dudley. p 125

6 December 1810. Tyra HARRIS and Patsey Butler, dau. of David Butler. Sur. William Butler. Tyra Harris is over 21 years of age. p 142

20 December 1807. Uriah HARRIS and Alice Johnson. Sur. John May. p 127

10 March 1814. John HARTSOOK and Sally Burton. Each party is 21 years of age. Sur. John S. May. Wit. John W. Cowherd. p 155

5 November 1794. William HARVIE and Frances Dear. Sur. Charles Dear. p 68

27 June 1792. William HARWOOD and Nancey White. Sur. John White, Jr. Married by Rev. William Douglas. p 58

29 January 1787. Elijah HAWKINS and Ann Hill. Sur. David Hill. Elijah was 21 years old in December 1785. p 34

5 December 1805. Elijah HAWKINS and Polly McCallester, in her 21st year, dau. of Elizabeth Armstrong. Sur. James G. Sharp. Wit. J. _____ Sharp. p 118

28 January 1783. John HAWKINS and Mary Garland Duke, dau. of Betty Duke. George Lumsden, Mary's guardian, consents for her. Sur. William P. Thurston. Wit. A. Parker, Martin Walton and John W. Pettus. p 22

16 December 1806. Anderson HAYNES and Peggy Swift, over 21 years of age, dau. of Richard Swift. Sur. Hezekiah Swift. p 123

9 February 1801. Christopher HAYNES and Joanah Perkins. Sur. William Perkins. Wit. William Dugan. p 97

11 December 1798. William HAYWOOD and Patsey Garth, dau.
of David Garth. Sur. Henry Garrett. Wit. William Garth
and John Fry. William is son of George Haywood. Married
by Rev. Richard Pope. p 86

10 January 1798. Christopher HENDERSON and Susanna Bourn,
dau. of Elizabeth Bourn. Sur. Adam Boyd. Wit. Lewis
Boarn. p 84

8 October 1792. Nathan HENDERSON and Mary Thomson. Sur.
James Hendrick. p 59

24 January 1803. John HENDRICK and Susanna Carpenter,
dau. of Philip Carpenter. Sur. Pleasant Carpenter.
Married by Rev. Richard Ferguson. p 105

19 December 1782. William HENDRICK and Ann Henderson.
Married by Rev. William Douglas. The Douglas Register
p 22

8 December 1793. Peter HENESSY and Winney Route. Married by Rev. John Lasley. Ministers' Returns p 364

7 April 1812. Richardson HENLEY and Judith Tisdale,
dau. of Shirley Tisdale. Sur. ___ ___. Married
by Rev. John Lasley. p 147

24 December 1807. Bartlett HENSON and Lucy Pulliam.
Sur. Isham Dashper. Married 25 December by Rev. John
Lasley. p 127

___ ___. John HESTER and Patsy Bibb. Sur. John
Bibb. Married by Rev. Richard Ferguson. Returned with
a group of marriages 19 August 1801. p 96

19 August 1779. John HESTER and Agnes Maifield. Sur.
James Tait. Married 26 August by Rev. William Douglas
who says Mayfield. p 12

11 February 1799. George HICKS and Lucy McGehee. Sur.
John McGehee. Married by Rev. Richard Ferguson who
says Hix. p 88

14 January 1799. Soloman HICKS and Judy Reynolds,
dau. of William Reynolds. Sur. David S. Hicks.
Soloman is son of David Hicks. Married 16 January by
Rev. William Baskett. p 87

17 March 1812. Benjamin HIGGASON and Jane T. Hollins,
over 21 years of age, dau. of Benjamin Hollins. Sur.
Richard Hollins. p 147

11 September 1786. Thomas HIGGASON and Ann White. Sur. John White. p 33

24 February 1795. Nathaniel HILL and Dicey King. Married by Rev. John Lasley. Ministers' Returns. p 368

25 December 1788. Samuel HILL and Nancy Tate. Married by Rev. William Douglas. The Douglas Register p 25

4 December 1801. Samuel HILL and Polley Peay. Sur. Nathan Sims. Wit. John Peay, Miley Peay and Richard Sims. (Milly?) p 99

20 June 1791. William HILL and Katharine Wasley. Robert Wasley gives consent for Katharine. Sur. David Hill. p 54

14 April 1813. Overton HINCHEE and Susan Brown. Sur. Richard Thompson. Wit. Augustine S. McGehee. Married by Rev. William Y. Hiter who says Susanna. p 152

13 December 1813. Pleasant HINCHEY and Eliza McGehee. (Also written Elizabeth McGehee on the bond). Sur. Richard Thompson. p 154

15 March 1797. John W. HINDE and Elizabeth Sydnor Marks, of age. Peter Marks makes affadavit that Elizabeth consents. Sur. Bickerton Winston. Married 16 March by Rev. H. Goodloe. p 81

10 February 1813. William Y. HITER and Jane Goodwin, dau. of Hugh Goodwin. Sur. James Beadles. Married 11 February by Rev. William Cooke. p 151

12 April 1790. James HOGAN and Mary Peers. Thomas Peers gives consent for Mary. Sur. William Mallory. Wit. Micajah Sims and Thomas Peers, Jr. p 50

19 April 1781. John HOGGAN and Elizabeth Pinax. Married by Rev. William Douglas. The Douglas Register p 21

12 October 1812. Micajah HOGG and Elizabeth Atkins. Sur. Hezekiah Atkins. p 149

22 February 1813. Austin HOGGARD and Salley Hambleton, dau. of David Hambleton. Sur. Joseph Boughan. Wit. William A. M. Hambleton and D. Hogard. Jesse Hogard consents for Austin. Married 23 February by Rev. William Cooke who says Salley H. Hambleton. p 151

11 November 1797. John HOGGARD and Betsey Smith. Sur. David Smith. Married 16 November by Rev. William Cooke. p 82

21 December 1795. John HOLLAND and Jane Tandy Rice,
dau. of Sary Rice. Sur. Zachariah Freeman. Wit.
Stephen Bourn. p 74

23 February 1776. Nathaniel HOLLAND and Jeanie Hutson.
Married by Rev. William Douglas. The Douglas Register
pp 17, 100

22 December 1806. Richard HOLLAND and Lucy Diggs, dau.
of Thomas Diggs who is surety. Richard is of Fluvanna
County. Married 23 December by Rev. William Baskett.
p 123

21 January 1799. Lewis HOLLIDAY and Catharine Boxley.
Sur. Thomas Boxley. Wit. Ralph S. Sandidge. p 88

31 July 1788. William HOLLIDAY and Rebekah Rowling.
Married by Rev. William Douglas. The Douglas
Register p 25

24 December 1807. George HOLLINS and Polley Edwards,
under 21 years of age, dau. of Reuben Edwards. Sur.
John Edwards. Married by Rev. John Lasley who says
George Holland. p 127

20 November 1805. Robert HOLLINS and Jane Fleeman.
Sur. John Fleeman. p 117

7 January 1793. William HOLLINS and Elizabeth Cole.
Sur. Benjamin Hollins. p 61

6 November 1799. James P. HOPKINS and Salley B. Brown.
William Smith makes affadavit that Salley is of age.
Sur. Thomas Smith. p 91

22 September 1784. John Christopher HORN and Sally
Thomson. Sur. John Thomson. Married 23 September by
Rev. William Douglas. p 26

9 March 1808. John HOUCHINS and Polly Cosby, dau. of
William Cosby. Sur. William Mallory. Wit. Robert
Harris. p 128

7 November 1810. Stephen HOUCHINS and Polly Chiles.
Sur. John Chiles. p 141

23 February 1791. Benjamin HOWARD and Milley Hunter,
dau. of Stephen Hunter. Sur. Nicholas Amos. Wit.
Salley Amous and William Purkins. Married 24 February
by Rev. John Lasley. p 53

9 June 1783. John HUGHES and Ann Meriwether, dau. of William Meriwether who is surety. Wit. Henry Wood and Vall. Meriwether. Married 18 June by Rev. William Douglas. p 23

2 November 1767. Joseph HUGHES and Mary Holland. Sur. Richard Holland. p 1

8 April 1811. William HUGHES and Martha Brooks. Sur. Henry Mallory. p 143

12 January 1808. James HUGHSON and Mary F. Kennon, dau. of John Kennon who is surety. Married 14 January by Rev. John Lasley. p 127

5 July 1815. William HUGHSON and Judith Henley. Sur. John Poindexter, Jr. Married by Rev. Claibourne Walton. p 158

27 December 1798. Duke William HULLUMS and Patsey McGehee. Sur. William McGehee? Married by Rev. Richard Ferguson. p 87

17 April 1799. Jesse HUMPHRESS and Sarah Landford, over 21 years of age. Sur. Wright Bond. Wit. Thomas Meriwether. Married 24 April by Rev. Richard Ferguson who says Lanford. p 89

4 May 1801. Isaiah HUMPHREY and Mary F. Walker. Sur. William Walker. p 98

3 January 1782. John HUMPHREYS and Sarah Young. Married by Rev. William Douglas. The Douglas Register p 21

12 December 1774. William HUMPHREYS and Sarah Stratham. Married by Rev. William Douglas. The Douglas Register p 15

25 October 1770. Andrew HUNTER and Ann Lane. Married by Rev. William Douglas. The Douglas Register p 12

8 January 1794. Forrest HUNTER and Janey Johnson, dau. of Elizabeth Johnson. Sur. Nuckolds Johnson. Married 12 January by Rev. Richard Pope who says Jancy. p 66

22 December 1803. George HUNTER and Elizabeth Morris. Sur. George Morris. p 109

9 February 1796. William HUNTER and Polley Morris. Sur. John Poindexter. p 75

8 November 1802. Arch^d. HUTCHINSON and Polley Crawford. Sur. John Crawford. Married 10 November by Rev. John Lasley who says Archibald Hutcheson. p 103

26 June 1788. David HUTSON and Mary Clapton. Married
by Rev. William Douglas. The Douglas Register p 25

26 December 1771. William IRVIN and Elizabeth Holt.
Sur. Joseph Holt. p 5

27 July 1804. Robert T. ISBELL and Martha H. Hope, dau.
of Benjamin B. Hope. Sur. Thomas Hope. Wit. Matthew
Hope and Frances J. Hope. p 112

29 June 1801. Major Charles JACKSON and Milley Anderson.
Sur. Nicholas Anderson. Wit. Sally M. Anderson. p 98

19 December 1809. John JACKSON and Mary Thompson.
Sur. William Mills, Jr. Wit. Ed. Banks and William
Mills, Sr. Married 21 December by Rev. William Cooke.
p 137

15 May 1804. Nelson JACKSON and Caty Fox, dau. of Grace
Fox. Sur. Meredith Fox. p 112

12 May 1806. Thomas JACKSON and Ann I. White. Sur.
Micajah Clark. p 121

14 June 1773. William JACKSON and Ann Johnson, dau. of
David Johnson. Sur. William Rice. p 7

28 February 1804. William JACKSON and Agnes A. Jackson,
dau. of Charles Jackson. Sur. Nelson Jackson. p 111

29 January 1808. Benjamin JENKINS and Anna Mansfield.
Sur. William Mansfield. Married 21 February by Rev.
Robert Jones. p 128

14 April 1781. Israel JENKINS and Ann Hollins. Sur.
Benjamin Hollins. Married 15 April by Rev. William
Douglas who says Ann Holland. p 17

10 March 1806. Daniel JENNINGS and Nancy Duval, dau. of
James Duval, deceased. Daniel Duval, of Culpeper
County, is Nancy's guardian. Sur. James T. Duval. Wit.
William Broadus, Jr. and Benjamin Duval. p 120

29 December 1802. John JENNINGS and Lucy Duvall, over
21 years of age. Sur. James T. Duval. Married by Rev.
Richard Pope. p 104

23 December 1805. William JENNINGS and Patsey Duval.
Sur. Benjamin Duval. Married 24 December by Rev.
Elisha Purington. p 119

27 September 1793. Francis JOHNSON and Barbara Hamilton
Mitchell, dau. of Thomas Mitchell. Sur. James Poindexter. p 63

20 October 1784. George JOHNSON and Jane Rowe. Sur.
Abraham Davis. Wit. William Henderson. Married 22
October by Rev. William Douglas who says Jean. p 27

9 December 1805. George H. JOHNSON and Elizabeth Hunter,
over 21 years of age. Sur. Richard Johnson. p 118

19 January 1784. Henry A. JOHNSON and Ann Michie. Sur.
John Poindexter, Jr. Married 20 January by Rev. William Douglas. p 25

15 May 1783. James JOHNSON and Sarah Bettesworth.
Married by Rev. William Douglas. (Tyler's Magazine
Vol. 6, p 24 says Butterworth). The Douglas Regis-
ter p 23

28 January 1778. James JOHNSON and Elizabeth Clarkson.
Sur. Ansellem Clarkson. Married by Rev. William Douglas. p 10

24 April 1790. James JOHNSON and Keziah Johnson, 'up-
wards of 21 years', dau. of David Johnson, deceased.
Sur. Joseph Isbell. Wit. John Johnson and Richard
Johnson. p 50

5 September 1796. John JOHNSON and Mary M. Daniel,
dau. of Mary Daniel. Sur. Josiah Davis. Wit. Ann
Daniel and Sarah Daniel. p 77

11 July 1801. John JOHNSON and Theodosia Gibson.
Sarah Gibson gives consent for Theodosia. Sur. Deamond
Harris. Wit. Martin Sharp. Married by Rev. Richard
Ferguson. Return is dated 19 August 1801. p 98

6 December 1796. John B. JOHNSON and Elizabeth Thomson,
dau. of Edward Thomson. Sur. John Thomson. Wit.
Richard Johnson and George Johnson, Jr. Married by Rev.
John Lasley. p 78

24 June 1789. Joseph JOHNSON and Sarah Freemen. Sur.
John Freeman. p 45

8 December 1804. Joseph F. JOHNSON and Delilah Hoggard,
dau. of Jesse Hogard. Sur. Andrew Kean. Wit. Nathaniel
Snelson, Martin Sharp and William Sharp, Jr. p 113

29 November 1785. Lewis JOHNSON and Massie Johnson,
dau. of James Johnson. Sur. Peter Crawford. Wit. John
Crawford. p 30

4 January 1788. Lewis JOHNSON and Barbary Garland, 21
years of age, dau. of Elizabeth Garland. Sur. John
Lane. Married 5 January by Rev. William Douglas who
says Barbara. p 38

14 March 1796. Lewis JOHNSON and Frances Winn. Sur.
John Badget. Wit. John Winn. Married 19 March by Rev.
Martin Walton. p 75

2 March 1796. Matthew JOHNSON and Betsey Porter, dau.
of Ebbin Porter. Sur. James Porter. Wit. John Bibb.
Married 3 March by Rev. John Lasley. p 75

16 October 1792. Nuckolds JOHNSON and Susannah Perkins.
Sur. John Purkins. p 59

13 February 1786. Phillip JOHNSON and Elizabeth White.
Sur. William White. p 31

2 March 1770. Richard JOHNSON and Susanna Garrett.
Sur. John Poindexter. p 2

30 September 1772. Richard JOHNSON and Ann Smith.
John Hawkins gives consent for each party. Sur. Wil-
liam Smith and Alexander Parker. Wit. Battaile Muse,
Samuel Clayton, Jr. and George Slaughter. p 6

21 February 1783. Richard JOHNSON and Lucy Hunter.
Sur. George Hunter. p 22

12 November 1806. Richard JOHNSON (2) and Susanna
Thacker, dau. of Mary Thacker. Sur. John Overton.
p 122

25 February 1799. Thomas JOHNSON and Nancey Price,
dau. of John Price. Sur. Jesse Perkins. Wit. David
Johnson. William Johnson is brother and guardian of
Thomas. Married 26 February by Rev. Richard Pope.
p 88

19 November 1799. Thomas JOHNSON and Nancey Johnson.
Sur. William Johnson. Married 20 November by Rev.
Richard Pope. p 91

11 April 1803. Thomas JOHNSON and Sally Poindexter.
Sur. Thomas Poindexter. Married 14 April by Rev.
John Lasley. p 106

4 February 1806. Thomas JOHNSON and Jane McDaniel.
Sur. John McDaniel. Married by Rev. John B.
Magruder of the Methodist Episcopal Church. Returned
21 March 1809. p 120

7 November 1768. William JOHNSON and Anne Clayton.
Sur. William Garrett, Jr. p 1

20 December 1793. William JOHNSON and Christian Smith,
dau. of William Smith who is bondsman and surety. Wit.
Ann M. Smith and Elizabeth Young Smith. Married 22
December by Rev. Martin Walton. p 64

10 February 1800. William JOHNSON and Frankey Beck.
Sur. Stanley Johnson. Married by Rev. Duke W. Hullum.
p 93

26 December 1810. William JOHNSON and Catharine Snelson,
dau. of Nathaniel Snelson. Sur. Francis Waldrop. p 142

9 February 1807. Anderson JONES and Nancy Bunch. Sur.
Anthony Bunch. Married 12 February by Rev. John Lasley.
p 125

8 April 1803. David JONES and Betsey Grubbs, dau. of
Matthew Grubbs. Sur. John Gray, Jr. Married 20 April
by Rev. Charles Hopkins. p 106

21 November 1810. David G. JONES and Roseanna Desper.
Overton Desper makes affadavit that Roseanna is over
the age of 21 years. Sur. Isham Desper. Married by
Rev. John Lasley who says Rosannah. p 141

16 November 1797. Drury JONES and Rebecca Moss. Sur.
Thomas Johnson. Married by Rev. Richard Pope. p 82

12 January 1809. John JONES and Frances Hope, dau. of
Benjamin B. Hope. Sur. Thomas Hope. Wit. Thomas A.
Hope. p 113

22 October 1792. Llewellin JONES and Mary Anderson,
dau. of Nelson Anderson. Sur. Alexander Anderson.
Wit. Martin Baker and Andrew Thomson. p 59

25 June 1789. Richard JONES and Jenny Edwards. Sur.
Gravet Edwards. Married by Rev. John Lasley. p 45

18 October 1814. Thomas JONES and Martha Lipscomb.
Sur. William T. Lipscomb or Tandy Lipscomb. p 156

1 August 1780. William JONES and Sally Thomas. Married by Rev. William Douglas. The Douglas Register
p 20

26 November 1799. John JURDEN and Sarah Martin. Married by Rev. William Baskett. Ministers' Returns p 372

14 September 1790. James KENNEDY and Barbara Smith,
dau. of George and Kezea Smith. (Keziah?) Sur. John
Smith. Wit. Barnett Smith. p 51

16 May 1793. Martin KENNEDY and Frances Smith, dau. of
Barnet and Jean Smith. Sur. John Smith. Wit. Tarleton
B. Luck. Married 23 May by Rev. Richard Pope. p 62

11 October 1810. Pleasant KENNON and Rebekah T.
Humphrey, over 21 years of age. Sur. Thomas Poindexter.
Married by Rev. John Lasley. p 140

16 March 1815. Pleasant KENT and Sally Reynolds,
(Sarey). Sur. George Ham. Wit. Philip Reynolds. p 157

14 January 1801. William KERR and Ciscelia Anderson.
Sur. Nicholas M. Anderson. p 97

14 June 1802. Anderson KERSEY and Salley Sims. Sur.
Nathan Tate. Returned 4 June 1803 by Rev. William
Cooke, p 101

12 December 1793. Claboarn KERSEY and Elizabeth
Edwards, dau. of Zachariah Edwards. Sur. Alexander
Kersey. Wit. Thomas Gardner. Married by Rev. Martin
Walton. p 64

1 March 1786. Elisha KERSEY and Mary Plant, dau. of
Williamson Plant, Sr. Sur. Williamson Plant, Jr.
Wit. Matthew Plant and George Kersy, Jr. p 31

11 March 1812. Garland KERSY and Polly Ryan. Sur.
William Tate. Married 26 March by Rev. William Cooke
who says Kersey. p 147

17 September 1781. George KERSEY, Junr. and Mary Hanes.
Sur. Nathan Anthony. Wit. Robert Sharp. p 18

20 January 1794. Meredith KERSEY and Lucy Pulliam,
dau. of Nathan Pulliam. Sur. Alexander Kersey. Wit.
Robert Pulliam. p 66

20 December 1793. Thomas KERSEY and Frances Ward,
dau. of William Ward. Sur. John Ward. Wit. Thomas
Gardner. Married by Rev. Martin Walton. p 64

1 May 1811. John KERSY, Junr. and Kitty Cauthon,
under the age of 21 years, dau. of William Cauthon.
Sur. Henry Kersy. Wit. Polley T. Kersey. John is
over the age of 21 years. Married 2 May by Rev.
William Cooke. p 144

17 March 1801. Jacob KIGER and Polly Davis, upwards of 21 years of age, dau. of Abraham Davis. Sur. George Johnson. Wit. James Breedlove, Married 19 March by Rev. William Cooke who says Kigo. p 97

14 January 1793. John KIMBROUGH and Jane Smith, (Jean), dau. of Barnet and Jean Smith. Sur. Joseph Kimbrough. Wit. John Moss. Married 20 January by Rev. Andrew Broaddus. p 61

27 November 1815. John KIMBROUGH and Catharine S. Boxley, dau. of John S. Boxley. Sur. Benjamin Boxley. Wit. William Boxley. Married 30 November by Rev. William Cooke. p 159

5 January 1785. Joseph KIMBROUGH and Elizabeth Yancy, dau. of Charles Yancey. Sur. John Poindexter, Jr. Wit. Unity Yancey and Rose Yancey. Married 6 January by Rev. William Douglas. p 27

5 January 1786. Robert KIMBROUGH and Sarah Smith, (Sally). Sur. John Poindexter, Jr. Wit. John Lipscomb and Rich^d. Paulett. Married 11 January by Rev. William Douglas. p 31

11 June 1795. Robert KIMBROUGH and Elizabeth Yancey. Sur. Charles Yancey. p 72

19 February 1805. William KIMBROUGH and Salley Smith. Sur. William Cooke. Wit. William S. Smith and Nelson Moss. Married 21 February by Rev. William Cooke. p 115

14 October 1789. Zachariah KING and Nancy Gunnell, dau. of William Gunnell. Sur. John Luck. p 46

8 May 1806. John KINNY and Nancey Captain, dau. of William and Lucy Captain. Sur. Reuben Flanagan. Wit. John Bourn. p 121

15 October 1780. Ephraim KNIGHT and Mildred Coaker. Married by Rev. William Douglas. The Douglas Register p 20

24 February 1782. William KNIGHTEN and Elizabeth Paterson. Married by Rev. William Douglas. The Douglas Register p 22

19 August 1795. James KNIGHTON and Barbara Hall, dau. of Elizabeth Hall. Sur. Lewis Sims. Wit. David Lanard and Mary Grady. Married by Rev. Martin Walton. p 72

21 March 1785. Thomas KNIGHTON, Jr. and Elizabeth Row.
Sur. John Hancock. Married 24 March by Rev. William
Douglas. p 28

28 July 1774. Charles LACY and Elizabeth Hudson. Married by Rev. William Douglas. The Douglas Register p 15

24 October 1787. Elijah LACY and Frankey Holland, dau.
of George Holland. Sur. Thomas Bell. Wit. Judith
Holland and Sally Holland. Returned 26 November by Rev.
H. Goodloe. p 36

6 September 1774. Jesse LACY and Mary Johnson. Married
by Rev. William Douglas. The Douglas Register p 15

21 July 1798. Kimbrough LANDERS and Keziah Humbles.
Sur. John Michie. Wit. Peter Crawford and Charles
Bibb. p 85

3 August 1791. James LANDRAM and Nancy Porter. Ebbin
Porter gives consent for Nancy and is surety. Wit.
James Porter and Daniel Landram. James is son of
Reuben Landram. p 55

2 December 1795. William LANDRAM and Mary Hubbard, dau.
of Daniel Hubbard. Sur. Carter Hubbard. Wit. Daniel
Landrum. p 73

15 May 1788. James LANDRUM and Peneay Watkins. Sur.
Isham Watkins. James was 21 years old July 1787.
Married by Rev. William Douglas. p 40

6 April 1801. Reubin LANDRUM and Martha Bibb. Sur.
William Bibb. Married 7 April by Rev. Duke W.
Hullum. p 97

12 May 1799. Thomas LANDRUM and Doney Parrish. Sur.
Joel Parrish. Married 14 May by Rev. John Lasley who
says Dolley. p 89

1 February 1781. John LANE and Ann Garland, dau. of
Nathaniel Garland. Sur. Garland McAllister. Married
6 February by Rev. William Douglas. p 17

2 August 1781. Richard LANE and Sarah Yancy. Sur.
Stephen Yancey. Married 9 August by Rev. William
Douglas. p 17

14 March 1796. Sharod LANE and Sarah Estis. Sur.
Joseph Doble. Married 16 March by Rev. Richard Pope
who says Sarah Estes. p 75

9 October 1797. James LANFORD and Nancy Edwards. Sur.
John Bibb. Married 12 October by Rev. John Lasley.
p 82

29 December 1803. John LANFORD and Polly F. Perkins,
dau. of John Perkins. Sur. William Garth. Wit. W. B.
Henley. Married by Rev. Duke W. Hullam. p 110

18 January 1810. Richard LANFORD and Caroline Matilda
Lasley, under age, dau. of John Lasley. Sur. John B.
Lasley, p 138

3 September 1793. Robert LANFORD and Patcy Bond. Sur.
Wright Bond. Married 5 September by Rev. Martin Walton
who says Patsey Bond, p 63

23 December 1811. John LASLEY and Susanna Perkins, dau.
of Joseph Perkins. Sur. Joseph Perkins, Jr. Married
24 December by Rev. John Owen who says John Lasly, Junr.
p 145

5 January 1797. Henderson LAWRENCE and Susanna Anderson,
dau. of Judith Anderson. Sur. John Lawrence. Married
6 January by Rev. Richard Pope. p 79

23 January 1809. Henry Lawrence and Mary Lipscomb.
Sur. Nicholas J. Poindexter. p 133

2 February 1795. John LAWRENCE and Sarah Anderson.
Judith Anderson gives consent for Sarah. Sur. Arch^s.
Anderson. Wit. Peter Bilbo. Married 4 February by
Rev. Richard Pope. p 70

5 November 1802. Richard LAYNE and Sarah Slayden.
William Slayden gives consent for Sarah. Sur. Aaron
Hall. Wit. Edward Dyhouse. Henry Layne, of Gooch-
land County, gives consent for Richard. Married 12
November by Rev. Lewis Chaudoin who says Richard
Lane. p 103

5 January 1797. John LEAK and Nancey Evans. Sur.
Emanuel Evans. Married 6 January by Rev. Richard
Pope. p 80

9 March 1789. John LEEK and Nancy Fleming. Married
by Rev. William Douglas. The Douglas Register p 25

13 September 1802. David LEMAY and Elizabeth H.
Johnson. Sur. Richard Johnson. Married by Rev.
Richard Pope. p 102

12 December 1791. Peter LESUEUR and Sarah Williams,
dau of John Williams. Sur. Benjamin Crenshaw, Jr.
Wit. Tabitha Crenshaw. p 57

9 November 1812. Nicholas H. LEWIS and Ann Meriwether.
Sur. James H. Terrell. Married by Rev. Jacob Watts.
p 149

18 December 1808. William LEWIS and Nancy Stevens, dau.
of John Stevens. Sur. William Stephens. Married by Rev.
John Lasley who says Nancey Stephens. p 132

2 May 1771. Major Zachariah LEWIS and Ann Terrill.
Sur. James Stevenson. Wit. Thomas Johnson, Gent.,
Elizabeth Tulloh and Ann Overton. p 4

8 November 1790. Armiger LILLY and Elizabeth Goldsmith.
Sur. John Bailey. Wit. James Armstrong and Lucy Armstrong. p 52

23 December 1799. Robert LILLY and Dicey Rice, born 13
October 1778, dau. of Sarah Rice. Sur. Matthew H. Rice.
Wit. Tarlton Rice. Married 26 December by Rev. William
Baskett. p 92

13 March 1815. Lunsford LINDSAY and Elizabeth Lipscomb,
dau. of David Lipscomb. Sur. Thomas H. Lipscomb. Wit.
Ira E. Lipscomb. Married by Rev. William Y. Hiter. p 157

7 June 1808. William LINNEY and Nancey White. Sur.
John White, Sen. p 129

2 February 1804. Barnabas LIPSCOMB and Polly Biggers,
dau. of Miles S. Biggers. Sur. William Thomson. Wit.
William Biggers. Married by Rev. D. W. Hullum who says
Mary Biggers p 110

10 December 1798. Henry LIPSCOMB and Frances Walton,
dau. of Mary Walton. Sur. John Walton. Wit. Joel
Walton. Married 13 December by Rev. Martin Walton.
p 86

18 December 1783. John LIPSCOMB, Jun[r]. and Salley
Smith, dau. of Edward Smith who is surety. p 24

16 November 1808. Waddy LIPSCOMB and Leticia Beadles.
Sur. James Beadles. Married 17 November by Rev.
William Cooke. p 131

20 December 1796. William LIPSCOMB and Ann Day Cooke,
dau. of William Cooke. Sur. David Lipscomb. Wit.
Thomas Lipscomb and A. Waller. Married 22 December by
Rev. William Cooke. p 78

1 December 1801. Garland LIVELY and Jane Wilkerson,
(Jean), of age. Sur. George Sims. Wit. Joseph
Eggleston. Married 3 December by Rev. William Cooke.
p 99

4 July 1797. John LOCKHARD and Frances Hall. Sur.
William Grady. Wit. William Mallory. Married 6 July
by Rev. Martin Walton. p 81

15 January 1784. Samuel LOGAN and Susannah Sharp, in
the 24th year of her age, dau. of Robert Sharp. Sur.
David Poindexter. Wit. William Sharp and James
Dabney. p 27

19 July 1808. John LONG and Susan Arnett. Sur. James
Arnett. Wit. Thomas Arnett. John is 21 years of age.
p 130

17 December 1805. Richard LOVING and Anne Wheeler.
Sur. John Wheeler. p 118

9 December 1805. William LOVING and Polly Robinson.
Sur. Stephen Williams. Wit. Lewis D. Collins. p 118

23 September 1800. John LOWRY and Catharine Gibson,
over 21 years of age. Sur. David Moore. Married 24
September by Rev. John Lasley. p 94

2 December 1797. Overton LOWRY and Nancy Thacker, dau.
of Isaac and Ann Thacker. Sur. Joseph Doble. Wit.
Anderson Thacker. Married 4 December by Rev. William
Baskett. p 83

10 December 1787. William LOWRY and Lucy Pulliam. Sur.
Thomas Dashper. Married 23 December by Rev. John
Lasley. p 37

14 May 1787. Thomas LUCAS and Martha Shelton. Sur.
John Bowen. Wit. J. Shelton and William Shelton, Jr.
p 35

16 August 1813. Augustine LUCK and Elizabeth Butler,
above 21 years of age. Sur. Garland Yancey. Wit.
Richard C. Eggleston. Married 17 August by Rev.
William Cooke. p 153

9 March 1789. John LUCK and Nancy Fleming, dau. of Ann
Fleming. Sur. William Spicer. Wit. Lindszey Arnold
and Richard Luck. John is son of Jesse Luck. p 44

11 April 1803. Overton LUCK and Caty Collins. Sur.
John Collins. p 106

13 March 1788. Richard LUCK and Mary Fleming, in the
19th year of her age, dau. of Ann Fleming. Sur. James
Sandidge. Wit. John Fleming, William Lumsden and
Thomas Lumsden. Richard is son of Jesse Luck. Married
14 March by Rev. William Douglas. p 40

22 December 1789, Tarlton B. LUCK and Crosha Cassity
Kennedy, upwards of 21 years, dau. of Crosha Kennedy.
Sur. James Kennedy. Married 24 December by Rev. John
Waller. p 48

15 May 1773. George LUMSDEN and Elizabeth Duke. Sur.
Cosby Duke. p 7

12 September 1797. Henry LUMSDEN and Susannah Matthews,
dau. of Eliza Matthews. Sur. George Lumsden. Wit.
Solomon Edwards. Henry is son of George Lumsden. Married 21 September by Rev. William Cooke. p 82

29 April 1803. Robert LUMSDEN and Mary Gunnell, over
21 years of age. Sur. John Tranham. p 106

25 January 1802. William LUMSDEN and Ann Young Cosby,
dau. of Wingfield Cosby. Sur. Charles Mills. Wit.
Thomas Cosby and George Lumsden. Married 28 January
by Rev. William Cooke. p 101

23 February 1777. Benjamin LYONS and Jeanie Hunter.
Married by Rev. William Douglas. The Douglas Register
p 17

7 April 1778. Rev. Daniel McALLA and Elizabeth Todd,
dau. of John Todd. Sur. Joseph Thomson. Rev.
McAlla's name is also written Daniel M. Calla on the
bond. p 10

18 February 1783. Alexander McALLISTER and Elizabeth
Smith. Sur. John Smith. Married 20 February by Rev.
William Douglas. p 22

18 August 1788. Benjamin McALLISTER and Lucy Faulkner.
Sur. Benjamin Hollins. Married 19 August by Rev. William Douglas. p 41

1 October 1808. James McALLISTER and Mary Cosby. Sur.
John Watkins and William Cole. Wit. Lydia Cole. p 130

10 March 1809. James McALLISTER and Mary Gooch. Sur.
Overton Gooch. Wit. Susan Gooch and Polly C. Cole.
p 134

22 March 1790. Nathaniel McALLISTER and Martha Johnson.
Sur. Abraham Davis. Wit. Ann Davis. Married by Rev.
William Douglas. p 49

5 December 1782. Alexander McCAULAY and Elizabeth Jerdone.
Sur. George Pattie. p 21

17 February 1780. John McCOY and Martha Humphreys.
Married by Rev. William Douglas. The Douglas
Register p 19

23 July 1792. Benjamin McDANIEL and Susanna Hughs.
Returned on the above date by Rev. Duke William Hullum.
(See Benjamin McDaniel). Ministers' Returns p 362

23 June 1799. Benjamin McDANIEL and Susanna Hughes.
Sur. William Faris. Wit. Alse Faris. (See Benjamin
McDaniel). p 89

14 October 1805. Chapman McDANIAL and Mary Whitlock,
dau. of Thomas Whitlock who is surety. Married by Rev.
John B. Magruder of the Methodist Episcopal Church.
Returned 21 March 1809. p 117

23 October 1792. William McDANIEL and Susanna Rowe,
of age, dau. of John Rowe. Sur. William Rowe. (See
William McDonald). p 60

29 November 1792. William McDONALD and Susannah Rowe.
Married by Rev. John Lasley. Ministers' Returns p 364
(See William McDaniel).

9 February 1790. Augustine McGEHEE and Sarah Thomson.
Sur. Benjamin Hollins. p 49

1 August 1812. Augustine S. McGEHEE and Mary M. Hester,
over the age of 21 years. Sur. Robert Hester. p 148

20 April 1815. Carr McGEHEE and Lucy Tate, dau. of
James Tate, Sr. Sur. Uriah Tate. Wit. William
Williams. Carr, under age, is son of John McGehee.
Married by Rev. William Y. Hiter. p 158

28 August 1781. Edward McGEHEE and Frances Lunsden.
Sur. George Lunsden. p 18

25 June 1808. George McGEHEE and Elizabeth G.
Nuckolls, dau. of Samuel Nuckolls. Sur. John L. Collins.
Wit. Elizabeth Collins and Mary Nuckolls. George is son
of W. McGehee. Married 5 July by Rev. William Cooke.
p 130

24 January 1775. John McGEHEE and Mary Stewart. George
Pottie gives consent for Mary. Sur. Charles Smith. p 9

25 October 1813. Oswell McGEHEE and Martha Cooke, over 21 years of age, dau. of W. Cooke. Sur. Edward N. Cooke. Wit. William Cooke, Jr. Married 30 October by Rev. William Cooke. p 153

9 February 1789. Samuel McGEHEE and Nancy Tate. Sur. ~~Zinvie (or Zinnie)~~ Tate. Married 12 February by Rev. John Lasley. p 43

19 November 1799. Thompson McGEHEE and Mary Thompson. Married by Rev. Richard Ferguson. Ministers' Returns p 373

24 December 1799. William L. McGEHEE and Mary Burruss, dau. of Ann Linney. Sur. Richard Bibb. Wit. David Biggers, Polly Biggers and William Arnett. Married 25 December by Rev. Richard Ferguson. p 92

9 January 1797. William McGEHEE and Nancy Bibb. Sur. John Bibb. p 80

9 March 1808. William McGEHEE and Barshaba Shirley. Sur. Richard McGehee. Wit. Susan McGehee. p 128

25 August 1808. Mattson McGHEE and Nancy P. Morris, dau. of George Morris. Sur. Dabney Morris. p 130

10 May 1787. William McGHEE and Ann Swiddy. Married by Rev. William Douglas. The Douglas Register p 24

1 January 1806. Charles MALLORY and Sarah Brooks, dau. of Lucy Brooks. Sur. William Brooks. Married 2 January by Rev. Elisha Purington. p 119

11 November 1805. Garland MALLORY and Susannah Brooks. Sur. William Brooks. Married _ November by Rev. Elisha Purington. p 117

15 June 1785. John MALLORY and Lucy Southerland, of age _ 22 years old, dau. of Joseph Southerland. Sur. Roger Mallory. Wit. Garrett Minor. p 29

28 December 1801. John MALLORY and Salley Mallory, dau. of Roger Mallory. Sur. John Mallory, Sr. Wit. William Pain and William Emmory. Married 29 December by Rev. Robert Jones. p 100

5 August 1790. George MALLORY and Elizabeth Bourn, dau. of Stephen Bourn. Sur. David Bourn. Wit. Thomas Green. p 50

28 February 1806. Minor MALLORY and Lucy King. Sur. Higgason King. p 120

4 October 1781. Thomas MALLORY and Constance Davis.
Married by Rev. William Douglas. The Douglas
Register p 21

13 November 1792. Thomas MALLORY and Ann Hoggard. Sur.
Jesse Hoggard. p 60

8 April 1805. Thomas MALLORY and Salley Mallory. Sur.
Henry Mallory. p 115

17 September 1807. William MALLORY and Lucinda Goodman.
Sur. Meriwether Smith. Wit. Abraham Collins. p 126

26 February 1803. William MALLORY, Jr. and Catharine
Harris, dau. of Nathan Harris. Sur. Edward Harris.
Wit. Samuel Harris. p 105

7 September 1790. Caleb MANDLEY and Ann White. Sur.
Daniel Bentley. Wit. John Perry and Elizabeth Perry.
Married 9 September by Rev. John Lasley. p 51

_____ _____ 1814. Arthur MANN and Martha Brown. Married
by Rev. William Y. Hiter. Ministers' Returns p 390
(See Arthur Mann).

27 April 1815. Arthur MANN and Marthey Brown. Sur.
Thomas Gunter. Wit. Wilson Ware. (See Arthur Mann)
p 158

9 December 1799. Richard MANTLO and Martha B. Harris.
Sur. Benjamin Harris. Married by Rev. Martin Walton.
p 91

22 July 1794. James MARTIN and Jane Stewart. Sur.
William T. Martin. p 67

19 September 1810. John MARTIN and Catharine Martin.
Sur. William Martin. Returned 30 October by Rev. W. E.
Waller. p 140

1 January 1807. Joseph MARTIN and Agatha Going, dau. of
Elizabeth Goin. Sur. William Smith who is bondsman.
Wit. Ambrose Flannagan and Whittle Flannagan. Married
2 January by Rev. John Lasley. p 124

12 November 1770. Thomas MARTIN and Ursley Clark who
gives her own consent. Sur. John Venable. Wit. Randal
Haley. p 3

21 March 1796. Jesse MASON and Polly Ann Branham. Sur.
Lawrence Mason. Wit. Thomas Mason. p 75

17 January 1794. Lawrence MASON and Rosanna Landers. Sur. Thomas Mason. Wit. James Kennedy and Thomas Mason, Jr. Lawrence is son of Thomas Mason. p 66

30 April 1783. Stephen THOMSON and Mary Armistead. Sur. Robert Armistead. p 22

26 November 1788. George MASSIE and Temprence Baker. Sur. James Pettit. Wit. Samuel Pettit. George is son of John Massie. p 42

24 November 1806. John MASSIE and Susanna Bibb, over 21 years of age, dau. of John Bibb. Sur. Thomas Bibb. p 122

9 November 1815. John MASSIE and Mary Walton. Sur. Martin Baker. Married by Rev. William Y. Hiter. p 159

20 May 1766. Thomas MASSIE and Mary Williams. Married by Rev. William Douglas. The Douglas Register p 9

30 November 1789. John MATHEWS and Susanna Wash, dau. of Mary Wash. Sur. John Fleming. Wit. Edward McGehee and Micajah Harris. p 47

21 November 1809. John W. MATHEWS and Polly Southworth, dau. of George Southworth. Sur. William Southworth. John is of Goochland County. Married 23 November by Rev. Lewis Chaudoin. p 137

5 December 1780. Zachariah MATLOCK and Lucy Wash. Sur. William Wash. Married 7 December by Rev. William Douglas. p 16

13 January 1791. Edward MATTHEWS and Martha Johnson. Edward is of Goochland County and Martha is of Fluvanna County. Married by Rev. John Lasley. Ministers' Returns p 363

23 April 1793. Richard MATTHEWS and Elizabeth Nelson. John Matthews makes affadavit that Elizabeth is over 21 years of age and he is surety. Married 29 April by Rev. Martin Walton. p 61

6 January 1779. Sharod MATTHEWS and Jane Byars. Sur. John Byars. Married 9 January by Rev. William Douglas who says Sharard and Jean. p 12

28 May 1782. James MAURY and Catharine Armistead. Sur. Robert Armistead. p 20

11 October 1791. Jeremiah MAY and Elizabeth Longest.
Sur. Abraham Pagget. Wit. Mary Padget and Faney
Longest. p 56

29 July 1784. Joel MAY and Jane Edrington. Sur. John
Edrington. p 26

13 May 1805. Samuel MAY and Elizabeth Shields. Sur.
Nathan Shields. Married 16 May by Rev. John Lasley.
p 116

3 May 1781. Henry MEAD and Frances Young. Married by
Rev. William Douglas. Ministers' Returns p 360

7 April 1798. Henry MEADE and Joannah Dickerson, dau.
of Rosanah Dickerson. Sur. George Dickerson. Wit.
Thornton Meade. p 84

9 April 1798. Henry MEAD and Elizabeth Dickerson.
Married by Rev. Jeremiah Chandler. Ministers'
Returns p 371

30 March 1790. William MEAD and Sarah Garland, dau. of
Elizabeth Garland. Sur. Jonathan Gordon. Married by
Rev. John Waller. p 50

18 January 1788. Thornton MEADE and Mary Garland.
Sur. William Meade. Wit. John Lane. Married 24
January by Rev. William Douglas. p 39

24 July 1809. Fielding MEADE and Mary Thacker. Sur.
James Hancock. p 136

27 March 1784. John MEED and Elizabeth Michie. George
Mickie is her guardian. Sur. Henry A. Johnson. Wit.
Henry Bibb and Minor Meed. Married by Rev. William
Douglas. p 25

6 January 1803. Bartlett MEEKES and Polly Cary, (Mary).
Each gives his or her own consent. Sur. Thomas Callis,
Jr. Wit. Stanley Alvis. Married 7 January by Rev.
William Cooke who says Mary Kersey. p 104

17 September 1805. William MEEKS and Hannah Rittenhouse,
over 21 years of age. Sur. William Crews, Sen[r]. Married 19 September by Rev. John Lasley. p 116

2 February 1797. Absalom MELTON and Nancy Freeman, dau.
of John Freeman. Sur. Josiah Freeman. p 80

11 May 1796. Austin MELTON and Susanna Baker. Sur.
John Freeman. p 76

8 November 1794. Thomas MELTON and Lydia McGehee, dau.
of James McGehee. Sur. John Arnett. Wit. William
Arnett and James McGehee, Jr. p 68

12 June 1809. Dr. William MEREDITH and Sarah F. Gardner,
dau. of Reuben Gardner of Hanover County. Sarah resides
with Thomas Gardner. Sur. Ben B. Ford. Wit. Robert
Meredith and John Talley. p 136

___ ___ 1815. Charles MERIWETHER and Ann Eliza
Anderson. Married by Rev. William Y. Hiter. Ministers'
Returns p 390

9 September 1784. James MERIWETHER and Sarah Meriwether,
dau. of William Meriwether who is surety. Wit. John
Poindexter, Jr. p 26

15 April 1771. John MERIWETHER and Easter McGehee, dau.
of William McGehee. Sur. John Whitton. John, under
age, is son of Francis Meriwether. p 4

18 September 1809. John MERIWETHER and Ann Tinsley.
Sur. William McGehee. p 136

1 June 1771. Nicholas MERIWETHER and Elizabeth
Meriwether. Sur. George Meriwether. p 4

9 January 1786. Nicholas MERIWETHER and Sarah Michie,
(Sally), 21 years of age, dau. of Elizabeth Ragland.
Sur. Waller Overton. Wit. John Michie. p 31

26 February 1787. Nicholas MERIWETHER and Beckey Terrell.
Sur. Richard Terrell. Married by Rev. William Douglas.
p 35

2 February 1798. Nicholas MERIWETHER and Mary Bickley,
over 21 years of age, dau. of John Bickley. Sur.
Richard Harris. Wit. Henry Garrett. Married 7 February by Rev. William Cooke who says Polly. p 84

19 July 1791. Thomas MERIWETHER and Ann Minor. Sur.
David Watson. p 55

13 February 1796. Thomas MERIWETHER and Polly Anderson.
Sur. George Poindexter. Wit. William G. Johnson. Married 17 February by Rev. William Cooke. p 75

14 December 1790. Valentine MERIWETHER and Priscilla
Pollard, under age, dau. of Thomas Pollard. Sur. James
Poindexter. Wit. Joseph Pollard, Jr., Robert Pollard
and David Bullock. p 52

14 July 1800. David MICHIE and Salley Michie. Sur.
Robert Michie. Wit. Nancey Michie. p 94

9 December 1780. James MICHIE and Sarah Ragland, dau.
of Samuel Ragland. Sur. John Nelson. Wit. Garland
Cosby and Martha Overton. p 16

17 January 1801. James MICHIE and Henrietta Ragland.
Sur. Thomas Meriwether. Wit. Richard C. Johnson and
Henry Lawrence. Married 19 January by Rev. John
Lasley who says Mickie. p 97

12 March 1804. Matthew MICHIE and Nancey Meade. Sur.
John Michie. Married by Rev. John Lasley. p 111

25 August 1812. Matthew MICHIE and Sarah Meade.
Ludwell Bramham is her guardian. Sur. Nicholas J.
Poindexter. Married 27 August by Rev. John Lasley.
p 148

6 January 1795. Patrick MICHIE and Dorothy Johnson,
dau. of Thomas Johnson, (Minister). Sur. James
Poindexter. Wit. George Poindexter. p 70

4 November 1781. George MICKIE and Elizabeth Mickie,
dau. of Robert Mickie. Sur. Thomas Moorman. Wit.
Thomas Puller. p 18

23 January 1790. John MICKIE and Lucy Mickie. Sur.
John Poindexter, Jr. Wit. William Michie, Matt
Mickie and Elizabeth Mickie. John is son of James
Mickie. p 48

2 October 1790. Henry MICKELBOROUGH and Elizabeth
Wilkerson. Sur. Richard Henley. Wit. John
Poindexter, Jr. p 51

1 August 1791. Isaac MILLAWAY and Sarah Faris. Sur.
Robert Taylor. Wit. Alexander Anderson. p 55

18 February 1807. James MILLS and Nancey B. Thomason.
Sur. George Thomason. p 125

5 April 1799. Jesse MILLS and Ann Phillips, widow.
William Barrett makes affadavit as to her age. Sur.
Charles Dabney, Jr. p 89

16 December 1807. Nathaniel MILLS and Catharine C.
Draper, dau. of Thomas Draper. Sur. Roger Burruss.
p 126

8 May 1769. Garrett MINOR and Mary Overton Terrill.
Ann and Richmond Terrill give consent for Mary. Sur.
James Overton. Wit. Charles Cosby and Fred Harris. p 2

10 May 1773. James MINOR and Mary Carr, dau. of John
Carr. Sur. Samuel Carr. Wit. Overton Carr and Vivion
Minor. p 7

27 July 1813. James MINOR and Mary Watson, (Polly),
dau. of James Watson. Sur. William Morris, Jr. Married by Rev. William Crawford, M. P. E. C. Returned
7 January 1815. p 152

14 June 1773. Vivion MINOR and Barbary Cosby. Sur.
Waller Overton. Wit. Garland Callis, James Cosby and
John Cosby. p 7

10 December 1798. William Snelson MITCHEL and Delpha
Mallory. Married by Rev. Reuben Ford. Ministers'
Returns p 372

26 December 1795. Archelaus MITCHELL and Patsey Terry,
dau. of Thomas Terry. Sur. Mills Terry. p 74

29 December 1801. Charles MITCHELL and Polley Garth.
Sur. William Haywood. Married 2 January 1802 by Rev.
John Lasley. p 100

13 September 1813. John E. MITCHELL and Nancy N.
Pulliam. Sur. William Chewning. p 153

4 July 1775. Thomas MITCHELL and Mildred Meriwether,
dau. of William Meriwether. Sur. George Meriwether.
Wit. John McGild or John W. Gill and John Harvie or
John Houre. p 10

29 April 1783. Thomas MITCHELL and Isabella Jerdone,
of age, dau. of Sarah Jerdone. Sur. John Nelson.
Wit. George Pottie. p 23

13 March 1802. John MONTAGUE and Molley Grady, dau.
of William Grady. Sur. Richmond Grady. Wit. James
Umpress. Married 18 March by Rev. William Cooke.
p 101

26 February 1785. Richard MOONEY and Sarah Price.
John Glenn gives consent for Sarah. Sur. David Garth.
Wit. John Donaleach(?). p 28

6 September 1790. James MOORE and Margaret Todd, dau.
of John Todd. Sur. Andrew Todd. Wit. Joseph Thomson.
p 51

21 April 1803. John MOORE and Elizabeth Humphrey,
(Betsey), dau. of Elijah Humphrey. Sur. Lewis
Humphrey. Wit. Jesse Humphrey and Henry Taylor.
Married by Rev. William Baskett. p 106

24 December 1798. James MOORMAN and Caty White, dau. of
William White. Sur. John White, Jr. Wit. Elizabeth
Cauthorn and Polly P. White. Married by Rev. Richard
Ferguson. p 87

3 June 1805. Robert MOORMAN and Dorothy Wash, dau. of
William Wash. Sur. Martin Wash. Wit. Robert Wash.
Married 4 June by Rev. John Lasley. p 116

10 February 1782. Thomas MOORMAN and Elizabeth Wash,
dau. of Mary Wash. Sur. William Wash. Wit. Robert
Anderson and James Moorman. p 19

31 December 1773. Zachariah MOREMEN and Elizabeth
Johnson. Sur. William Davis. p 8

12 August 1809. Dickerson MORRIS and Nancey L. Young.
Sur. Thomas Turner. p 136

21 July 1783. George MORRIS and Salley Bigger. William
Bigger gives consent for Salley. Sur. James Bigger.
Married 11 September by Rev. William Douglas. p 23

7 November 1808. George MORRIS and Martha Lea, dau.
of John Lea. Sur. Joshua Morris. Married 10 November by Rev. William Baskett. p 131

1 October 1799. Guttrey MORRIS and Dolley Holland,
dau. of Hezekiah Holland. Sur. John Holland. p 90

20 December 1783. Isaac MORRIS and Ann Dickerson
Smith, dau. of Nathan Smith who is surety. Married
23 December by Rev. William Douglas. p 24

23 February 1791. John MORRIS and Lucy Walker, dau.
of Sarah Walker. Sur. Thomas Dunn. Wit. John
Poindexter. p 53

27 August 1791. Samuel MORRIS and Martha Biggers.
Sur. John Maddison. Married by Rev. William Douglas.
p 56

18 August 1782. Thomas MORRIS and Mary Russel. Married by Rev. William Douglas. The Douglas Register
p 22

20 January 1801. William MORRIS, Jr. and Nancey Watson,
dau. of James Watson. Sur. Richard Morris. Wit. Polly
Watson. p 97

21 December 1801. Joshua MORRISS and Nancy Lea, dau.
of John Lea. Sur. George Morriss. p 100

9 April 1773. Joseph MORTON and Mary Ragland, dau. of
William Ragland. Sur. John Hawkins. Wit. John Robinson,
Ben. Hawkins and John Bourn. p 6

22 April 1771. Benjamin MOSBY and Ursuly Clark. Sur.
Harry Pryor. p 4

31 December 1779. David MOSBY and Ann Cock. Sur.
Robert Mosby. p 14

8 September 1786. Benjamin MOSS and Elizabeth Gregson.
Sur. John Yancey. Wit. Susan^n Wash and George Lunsden.
p 33

10 November 1794. Benjamin MOSS and Susannah Wash.
Sur. John Poindexter, Jr. Wit. George Lumsden. Married 13 November by Rev. William Cooke. p 69

21 March 1767. John MOSS and Sarah Kimbrow, (widow).
Sur. William Snelson, Jr. p 1

20 June 1808. John MUNDAY and Elizabeth Burrus, dau.
of John Burrose. Sur. Henry Burras. John Munday is
of Albemarle County. p 129

31 December 1808. John MUNDAY and Nancey Lane. Sur.
Henry Edwards. p 133

28 April 1794. Thomas NAPIER and Mary Ratliff, Sur.
Kimbrough Landers. Married by Rev. John Lasley who
says Napper. p 67

10 October 1795. James NELSON and Mary Overton. Sur.
James Overton. Married 14 October by Rev. William
Cooke. p 73

9 November 1796. James NELSON and Elizabeth Gooch,
dau. of Stephen Gooch who consents and is surety. p 78

11 July 1808. John NELSON and Jane Wright, over 21
years of age. Sur. Richard Wright. p 130

12 March 1804. John T. NELSON and Elizabeth Hester,
dau. of John Hester, Sr. Sur. John Hester, Jr. Wit.
Robert Hester. Married 21 March by Rev. D. W.
Hullum. p 111

29 May 1773. Joseph NELSON and Lucy Tate, dau. of
William Tate, Sr. Sur. Robert Tate. Wit. John
Hawkins, Sr. p 7

14 April 1788. William NELSON and Elizabeth Robinson,
dau. of William Robinson. Sur. Samuel Robinson. Wit.
Francis Robinson. p 40

16 June 1802. William T. NELSON and Matilda Tate, dau.
of James Tate. Sur, Cornelius Gooch. Married by Rev.
Richard Ferguson. Returned 1 May 1804. p 101

29 February 1789. Samuel NICHOLS and Sarah Garland.
Married by Rev, William Douglas. The Douglas Register
p 25

26 September 1782. William NICHOLS and Henrietta Terry.
Married by Rev. William Douglas, The Douglas Register
p 22

16 November 1813. Benjamin NIGHT and Elizabeth Bunch.
Married by Rev, John Lasley. Ministers' Returns .p 389

10 January 1803. John NORMAN and Sarah Mann, over 21
years of age. Sur. William Eddes. p 105

24 October 1788. James NORTON and Jane Bybe. Married
by Rev. John Lasley. Ministers' Returns p 361

15 July 1780. Hugh NORVELL and Jane Duncan. Sur.
Robert Duncan. p 15

26 September 1785. Nathaniel NUCKOLDS and Henrietta
Garland, 21 years of age, dau. of Robert Garland. Sur.
John Nuckolds. Wit. Robert Garland, Jr. p 29

13 February 1809. James D. NUCKOLLS and Frances S.
Thomasson. Sur. John Thomasson. p 134

7 October 1800. Nathaniel NUCKOLLS and Patsy Towler,
over 21 years of age. Sur. James Hughson. Also on
the bond is Patsy Toler. Married 9 October by Rev.
William Cooke who says Toler. p 95

14 September 1789. Richard NUCKOLLS and Temperance
Walton. Sur. Robert Barrett. Returned 1 November by
Rev. John Waller. p 46

26 February 1789. Samuel NUCKOLLS and Sarah Garland.
Sur. John Nuckolls. Married 29 February by Rev.
William Douglas who says Nichols. p 44
(1789 was not a 'Leap Year' -- I think this should be
28 February. However '29 February' is in The Douglas
Register on page 25).

24 September 1782. William NUCKOLLS and Henneritter
Terry, dau. of James and Henneritta Terry. Sur. James
Nuckolls. Wit. David Bullock, William Pope and Richard
Nuckolls. Married 26 September by Rev. William Douglas
who says Nichols and Henrietta. p 20

20 June 1815. Lewis NUCKOLS and Eliza C. Maddison.
Sur. William Dickinson. Married by Rev. William Cooke.
p 158

12 January 1804. Reuben NUCKOLS and Polley Duke. Sur.
Hardin Duke. Reuben, son of Pouncey Nuckols, is under
age. p 110

4 March 1785. Thomas NUCKOLS and Ann Terry. Henrietta
Terry gives consent for Ann. Sur. William Nuckolls.
p 28

3 October 1811. John NUNN and Polly Harris. Sur.
Arthur Clayton. Wit. William Thomson, Jr. p 144

25 October 1813. James OLIVER and Nancey Humphrey.
Sur. Lewis Humphrey. Wit. Benjamin Davis. p 153

22 February 1795. John OMOHUNDER and Nancy Crank, dau.
of George Crank. Sur. William Terry. Wit. William
Pettit. Married 26 February by Rev. William Cooke who
says Omohundro. p 71

4 March 1779. Jacob ORFORD and Nancy HUNTER. Married
by Rev. William Douglas. The Douglas Register p 18

22 December 1800. Richard OVERTON and Salley Johnson.
Sur. William G. Poindexter. Married by Rev. Richard
Pope. p 96

9 March 1799. Waller OVERTON and Martha Ragland,
dau. of Samuel Ragland. Sur. Garritt Minor. Wit.
James Overton, Jr. p 12

10 November 1810. Bernard OWENS and Elizabeth Gardner,
over 21 years of age. Sur. Reuben Gardner. Wit.
Bernard Owens and Nancy Gardner. Married 22 November
by Rev. W. E. Waller. p 141

16 February 1813. David OWIN and Ann Gardner. Sur.
James Gardner. Married 25 February by Rev. William
Cooke who says Owens. p 151

22 October 1806. Elisha PACE and Patsy Johnson, dau.
of Thomas Johnson. Sur. Stanhope Johnson. Wit.
Thomas Johnson, Jr. p 122

24 September 1793. Ephraim PAGGETT and Fanny Thacker,
of age. Sur. Charles Bibb. Wit. Masey Thacker. p 63

15 January 1810. Lewis PAGGETT and Elizabeth Gentry,
dau. of Fanney Gentry. Sur. Thomas Mann. Married 16
January by Rev. John Lasley. p 138

28 March 1796. John PAINTER and Patsy Thomson. Sur.
Charles Thomson. Married by Rev. John Lasley who says
Patsey Thompson. p 76

9 November 1812. Fleming PARISH and Mary Grubbs, (Nancy),
dau. of Matthew Grubbs. Sur. Richard Wright. Wit.
William L. Jones. p 149

11 October 1780. James PARISH and Sarah Timberlake.
Married by Rev. William Douglas who spells it
Timberlick. The Douglas Register p 20

28 December 1792. Park PARISH and Elizabeth Tisdale.
Sur. Joel Parrish. Wit. John Allen. p 60

2 December 1773. William Lowe John PARK and Mourning
Fleming. Sur. Carr Smith. Wit. John Smith. p 7

3 November 1770. Alexander PARKER and Sarah Smith.
John Hawkins and William Smith give consent. Sur.
Robert Stubblefield. Wit. Joseph Hawkins, Lucy Duke,
Clevears Duke and Beverly Stubblefield. Alexander is
son of William Parker. p 3

4 December 1788. Mager PARRISH and Judith Shelton,
dau. of Peter Shelton. Sur. John Austin. Wit. Daniel
Shelton and Thomas Shelton. Mager is of Goochland
County. (Major?) p 42

28 December 1803. Nelson PARRISH and Elizabeth C.
Spencer. Sur. William Graven. Married 30 December
by Rev. Elisha Purington. p 110

26 February 1810. Zachariah PARRISH and Susanna White,
over 21 years of age. Sur. Thomas Mann. p 139

2 January 1783. Tyree PARROT and Olney Bowe. Married
by Rev. William Douglas. The Douglas Register p 22

12 May 1800. William PARROTT and Elizabeth Peed,
(Betsey). Sur. Cyrus Peed. Wit. Nancy Peed. William
is son of John Parrott. p 93

12 December 1805. Augustus PARSONS and Elizabeth
Britton. Sur. John N. Christmas. Married by Rev.
Charles Hopkins. p 118

7 March 1789. Samuel PARSONS and Catharine Plant, upwards of 21 years. Sur. Thomas Kersey. Wit. Harden
Duke. Returned 23 August by Rev. Charles Hopkins. p 44

12 December 1808. Austin PATE and Agatha Stanley, over
21 years of age. Sur. George Strong. Married 15
December by Rev. William Cooke. p 132

27 December 1779. John PATTERSON and Elizabeth Maria Meriwether. George Meriwether makes affadavit as to Elizabeth's age. Sur. William Steel. p 14

14 September 1801. William PATTERSON and Caty Trower, dau. of Solomon Trower. Sur. Henry Trower. Wit. Samuel Overton. p 99

8 February 1774. William PAULET and Sarah Watson. Sur. William Lipscomb. p 8

8 January 1781. Richard PAULETT and Catharine Smith. Sur. Obediah Trimmer. Married 10 January by Rev. William Douglas. p 17

2 January 1812. Benjamin PAYNE and Polly Walker, dau. of William Walker. Sur. William Allen. p 146

11 December 1815. Thomas G. PAYNE and Susanna Walker. Sur. Horace Timberlake. p 160

12 October 1801. Anthony PEAY and Babby Sims. Sur. Fenton Sims. p 99

10 February 1798. Thomas PEERS, Jr. and Elley Parsons, dau. of Samuel Parsons. Sur. John N. Christmas. Wit. Lydall Britton and Judeth Parsons. p 84

22 May 1799. William PEERS and Elizabeth Freeman. Sur. Robert Freeman. Married 24 May by Rev. Richard Pope. p 89

20 February 1793. Abisha PEMBERTON and Cynthia F. Parish, dau. of Ann Parish. Sur. Corbin Parish and Corbin Parish. p 61

8 February 1808. Edmund PENDLETON and Unity Y. Kimbrough. R. Yancey is Unity's guardian. Sur. Peter Barrett. Wit. John Edwards. p 128

25 October 1785. Henry PENDLETON and Alice Ann Winston. Robert Barrett gives consent for Alice Ann. Sur. Elijah Dickinson. Wit. John Poindexter. p 29

10 July 1792. Elisha PENINGTON and Sarah Todd, dau. of John Todd who is surety. p 58

25 December 1780. Antony PERKINS and Aggie Pulham. Married by Rev. William Douglas. The Douglas Register p 20

16 December 1805. John B. PERKINS and Lucy Mallory, dau. of Henry Mallory. Sur. Thomas Hughes. Married by Rev. Elisha Purington. p 118

15 December 1808. Knight B. PERKINS and Rebecca Mallory, dau. of Henry Mallory. Sur. William Brooks. Wit. Salley Mallory and Joseph Perkins. Stephen Perkins gives consent for Knight B. who is of Fluvanna County. p 132

21 February 1784. Samuel PERKINS and Jean Johnson, dau. of Richard Johnson. Sur. Charles Thomas. Wit. Richard Johnson, Jarriot Wilkerson and John Price. Samuel Perkins is son of John Purkins. p 25

13 August 1785. William PERKINS and Martha Hunter, dau. of Stephen Hunter. Sur. William Harris, Jr. Wit. Bartlet Haley and Edward Eastham. p 29

8 January 1807. William PERKINS and Frances C. Bowls. Married by Rev. John Lasley. Ministers' Returns p 382

12 October 1784. Bartlet PERRY and Mary Simson. Married by Rev. William Douglas. The Douglas Register p 23

2 October 1789. John PERRY and Elizabeth Chandler. Sur. James Poindexter. Married by Rev. John Lasley. p 46

4 October 1800. William PERRY and Susanna Dickinson. Sur. Thomas Dickinson. Wit. Abram Baskett. Married by Rev. Richard Pope. p 95

3 August 1785. James PETTIT and Frances Baker. Sur. William Baker. p 29

17 December 1793. William PETTIT, Jr. and Frances Crank, dau. of George Crank. Sur. Lipscomb Crank. Wit. William Pettit. p 64

22 December 1789. Samuel Baker PETTIT and Temperance Sharp, dau. of William Sharp and sister of Thomas Sharp who is surety. Wit. William Pettit. p 48

13 October 1795. Hart O. PETTUS and Barbara Pettus. Married by Rev. William Cooke. Ministers' Returns p 367

12 December 1796. Joseph PETTUS and Lucy Graves, dau. of Rice Graves. Sur. John Graves. Wit. Benjamin Graves. p 78

14 September 1795. Overton H. PETTUS and Barbara Cosby, dau. of Wingfield Cosby. Sur. John Toler. p 73

9 February 1784. William PETTUS, Jr. and Lucy W. Pettus. William Pettus is guardian of Lucy. Sur. Clevears Duke, Jr. Wit. James Overton and W. Wright, Jr. William is son of William Pettus, Sr. p 25

15 November 1785. Richard PHILLIPS and Elizabeth Waddy.
Sur William Phillips. p 30

30 August 1802. Thomas PHILLIPS and Catharine Phillips.
Sur. Francis Anderson. p 102

29 December 1798. Jennings PLANT and Susannah Richardson,
dau. of Richard Richardson. Sur. Matthew Plant. Wit.
Liney Richardson. Married 30 December by Rev. Martin
Walton. p 87

17 February 1787. Matthew PLANT and Mourning Hambleton,
dau. of Sarah Hambleton. Richard Richardson, Mourning's
guardian, consents. Sur. James Poindexter. Wit. Thomas
Christmas and Williamson Plant. p 34

2 May 1801. Thomas E. PLEASANTS and Jane Chewning, dau.
of Jane Chewning. Sur. Reubin Chewning. p 98

9 January 1792. Charles POINDEXTER and Sarah May. Sur.
James Beadles. p 57

16 March 1787. David POINDEXTER and Frances Pope
Johnson. G. Johnson gives consent for Frances. Sur.
John Chisholm. p 35

16 August 1810. James POINDEXTER and Patsey West. Sur.
Nicholas J. Poindexter. Wit. Mary W. Beadles and Fanny
Dickinson. p 140

14 July 1785. John POINDEXTER and Frances Arnet.
Married by Rev. William Douglas. The Douglas Register
p 24

17 December 1781. John POINDEXTER and Elizabeth
Thornton Johnson. Sur. Jesse Paulett. p 18

9 August 1815. John POINDEXTER, Jr. and Elizabeth
Graves. Sur. William Anderson. Married by Rev. William
Y. Hiter. p 159

12 September 1803. Joseph POINDEXTER and Rody May.
Sur. Samuel May. p 108

17 December 1806. Nicholas J. POINDEXTER and Rebecca
Ragland. Sur. Micajah Clarke, Jr. Married 18 December
by Rev. John Lasley who says Nicholas Johnson Poindexter.
p 123

11 _____ 1786. Peter POINDEXTER and Lucy Arnett. Sur.
James Trice. p 31

24 March 1790. Thomas POINDEXTER and Sarah Ragland, dau. of William Ragland. Sur. John Mickie. Wit. Salley Ragland. Married 28 March by Rev. John Lasley. p 49

24 August 1791. William POINDEXTER and Polley McGehee, dau. of William and Pattey McGehee. Bondsman, V. Poindexter. p 56

10 January 1781. Richard POLLET and Catie Smith. Married by Rev. William Douglas. Ministers' Returns p 360

11 October 1806. Thomas POORE and Jane Drake, dau. of John Lea who is surety. p 122

14 January 1793. James PORTER and Lydda Wasley. Sur. Ebben Porter. Married 31 January by Rev. John Lasley p 61

19 June 1782. William PORTER and Sarah Johnson. Sur. James Barnet. Married 20 June by Rev. William Douglas p 20

8 October 1771. George POTTIE and Mary Jerdone, dau. of Sarah Jerdone. Sur. John Marshall. p 4

16 August 1799. Daniel POWERS and Salley Ryan, over 25 years of age, sister of John Ryan. Sur. Benjamin Howard. Wit. John Ryan, Kittner Ryan and Benjamin Howard. Married 17 August by Rev. Richard Pope. p 90

18 July 1775. David POWERS and Elizabeth Laurence. Married by Rev. William Douglas. The Douglas Register p 16

14 March 1811. Thomas POWERS and Elizabeth King, over the age of 21 years. Sur. William Mallory. Married 16 March by Rev. William Cooke. p 143

9 December 1812. Thomas POWERS and Salley Wright. Sur. John Wright. Married 17 December by Rev. William Cooke. p 149

10 August 1801. William PRICE, Jr. and Nancey Haywood. Sur. Moses Bates. William, Jr. is son of John Price. Married 11 August by Rev. Richard Pope. p 98

24 January 1815. William W. PRICE and Dorothy A. Trice, dau. of James Trice. Sur. Tarleton Henley. Wit. Dorothy Anderson. William is over 21 years of age. p 157

8 August 1808. Wilson PRICE and Ann Smith, dau. of William Smith. William Price gives consent for Wilson. Sur. Zachariah W. Perkins. Wit. William Price, Jr. p 130

28 December 1811. Cain PRIDDY and Nancy McDaniel, over 21 years of age, dau. of John McDaniel. Sur. Thomas Johnson, Jun[r]. Wit. John Priddy and Sally McDaniel. p 146

1 November 1790. John PRIDDY and Martha Rowe, upwards of 21 years of age, dau. of Lucy Rowe. Sur. Charles Hunter who made oath as to Martha's age. Wit. Thomas Johnson. p 51

31 August 1795. Larkin PRIDDY and Mary Hunter. Sur. Samuel Hunter. p 72

19 July 1778. Thomas PULHAM and Jean Ray. Married by Rev. William Douglas. The Douglas Register p 18

14 February 1782. Zachariah PULHAM and Sarah Black. Married by Rev. William Douglas. The Douglas Register p 21

11 April 1793. John PULLIAM, Jr. and Salley Perkins. Sur. Edward Furr. Married by Rev. Richard Pope. p 61

31 January 1778. William PULLIAM and Mourning Richardson, dau. of Richard Richardson. Sur. Beverley Glenn. Wit. David Sims, John Richardson and John Mayo. p 10

18 June 1798. Samuel PURKINS and Susanna Pass, over 21 years of age. Sur. John Thomas. Wit. Jesse Chewning. Married 20 June by Rev. Richard Pope. p 85

13 March 1803. William PURKINS and Matilda Gentry. Sur. John Gentry. Wit. William Dugins. Married 17 March by Rev. William Cooke. p 106

8 February 1802. Captain Charles QUARLES and Ann Mills, dau. of William Mills. Sur. W. G. Poindexter. Married by Rev. Richard Ferguson. Returned 1 May 1804. p 101

2 October 1813. Garrett M. QUARLES and Mary Poindexter. Sur. Nelson B. Barret and John Poindexter, Jr. Married by Rev. William Y. Hiter. p 153

16 November 1791. John QUARLES and Rebecca Minor, (Becky), dau of Garrett Minor. Sur. Robert Quarles. p 56
(Is this a double wedding? See Robert Quarles)

16 November 1791. Robert QUARLES and Patsey Minor, dau. of Garrett Minor. Sur. John Quarles. (Is this a double wedding? See John Quarles.) p 57

20 December 1793. William QUARLES and Lucy Johnson.
Sur. Joseph Winston. p 65

11 December 1788. Samuel RAGLAND and Elizabeth Mickie.
Sur. John Mickie. Married 12 December by Rev. William
Douglas who says Raglin and Meekie. p 43

18 December 1779. Nathaniel RAINE and Judah Blackwell.
Sur. Thomas Shelton. Wit. Thomas Terrell. Married 19
December by Rev. William Douglas who says Judith. p 13

3 December 1800. Thomas H. RATLIFF and Lucey Johnson,
dau. of Lucey Johnson. Sur. Richard Jones. Wit.
Ursula Estis. Married 4 December by Rev. John Lasley.
p 96

19 March 1810. Peyton J. RAWLINS and Lucy J. Winston,
dau. of Joseph Winston. Sur. John J. Winston. Married
20 March by Rev. William Cooke. p 139

17 March 1794. John REANER and Lucy Stowers, 21 years
of age. Sur. John Thomson. p 66

15 March 1785. Abraham REDMAN and Elizabeth Slater.
Sur. William Settle. Wit. John Hawkins. Married 17
March by Rev. William Douglas. p 28

23 November 1787. Abraham REDMAN and Catharine Brown.
Sur. Robert Wasley. Wit. John Poindexter. Married by
Rev. William Douglas. p 37

5 February 1789. Benjamin RENOLDS and Elizabeth Fleeman.
Sur. John Fleeman. Married by Rev. William Douglas who
says Fleming. p 43

12 October 1801. Austin REYNOLDS and Anne Fulcher.
Sur. John Fulcher. Married 13 October by Rev. John
Lasley. p 99

21 March 1803. Charles REYNOLDS and Dolly Dickason,
dau. of Zachariah Dickason. Sur. David Dickason. Wit.
Eleven Smith. Married 24 March by Rev. William
Baskett. p 106

14 May 1795. George REYNOLDS and Elizabeth Beckley.
Sur. David Reynolds. Married by Rev. John Lasley who
says Bickley. p 71

12 March 1800. John REYNOLDS and Polley Gilbert. Sur.
John Gilbert. Married by Rev. William Baskett. p 93

5 February 1812. John Thornton REYNOLDS and Polley
Watkins, dau. of Thornton Gibson. Sur. Reuben Reynolds.
Wit. Taliaferro Reynolds. p 146

29 November 1802. Joseph REYNOLDS and Polly Dashper.
Sur. Philip Reynolds. Wit. Clyton R. Henson and
Nathaniel Bunch. p 103

7 November 1796. Phillip REYNOLDS and Nancy Seargeant.
Sur. William Seargeant. Married 9 November by Rev.
William Baskett. p 78

16 January 1805. William REYNOLDS and Elizabeth Gilbert,
dau. of John Gilbert, Sr. Sur. Cosby Duke. Married 17
January by Rev. John Lasley. p 115

23 December 1805. William REYNOLDS, Jr. and Mary Lemay,
dau. of Charles Lemay, deceased. Sur. Cosby Duke.
Married 28 December by Rev. John Lasley. p 119

21 December 1808. Charles RICE and Sarah Lipscomb.
Sur. Joseph Terry. Wit. John Thompson. Married 22
December by Rev. William Cooke. p 132

22 March 1808. Tarlton RICE and Elizabeth Lea (Betty
Jane), dau. of John Lea. Sur. Thomas Freeman. Wit.
Patsey Lea. Tarlton is of Fluvanna County. Married 24
March by Rev. William Baskett. p 129

27 December 1808. William RICE and Jane Walker. Married
by Rev. John Lasley. Ministers' Returns p 384

10 October 1810. David RICHARDSON and Jane Anthony,
under age, dau. of Nathaniel Anthony. Sur. Jennings
Plant. Married 11 October by Rev. William Cooke. p 140

22 March 1809. John RICHARDSON and Sally Hollins, dau.
of Benjamin Hollins. Sur. William Hollins. Wit.
Richard Hollins. p 135

12 January 1807. Lindsay RICHARDSON and Lucy Marks,
alias Lee. Sur. Thomas Sledd. p 124

3 December 1782. Robert RICHARDSON and Mary Bibb. Sur.
William Biggar, Junr. p 21

1 December 1770. Samuel RICHARDSON and Ann English who
gives her own consent. Sur. James Johnson. Wit.
George Thompson. p 3

10 February 1784. William RICHARDSON and Nancy Arnett.
Sur. James Arnett. Married 11 February. No Minister's
name is given. p 25

22 February 1776. William RIGSBY and Susannah Adams.
Married by Rev. William Douglas. The Douglas Register
p 17

17 July 1788. Jesse ROBARDS and Jrances A. Perkins, dau. of Joseph Perkins. Sur. George Robards. Wit. Robert Perkins. p 41

24 February 1810. Jeremiah ROBERTS and Polly Chewning. Sur. Joseph Chewning. p 139

April 1779. William ROBERTS and Sarah Hutson. Married by Rev. William Douglas. The Douglas Register p 19

2 February 1798. Martin ROBERTSON and Sarah Morton, dau. of William J. Morton. Sur. William G. Poindexter. Married 6 February by Rev. Richard Pope. p 84

13 June 1774. Stephen ROBINSON and Betty Holland, dau. of George Holland. Sur. Thomas Johnson, Jr. Wit. James Coleman, Ann Howle and James Johnson. p 8

22 February 1806. William P. ROBINSON and Jane Drake. John Lea gives consent for Jane. Sur. Pleasant Farley. p 120

9 August 1798. Richard ROCHE and Nancy Rittenhouse, of full age. Susanna Rittenhouse consents for Nancy. Sur. Samuel Rittenhouse. Wit. Matthew Bellomy. Married 10 August by Rev. William Baskett. p 85

22 August 1789. Walter RODES and Elizabeth Thomson. Sur. John Thomson. p 46

25 April 1791. John ROGERS and Sarah Tunstall. Sur. Joseph Tunstall. p 54

1 September 1803. Lewis ROGERS and Polly Shepard, dau. of James Shepard. Sur. Thomas Rogers. Wit. William Lovell. James Shepard is of Goochland County. Polly resides with her sister, Elizabeth, wife of William Lovell. p 107

24 September 1792. Alexander ROSBERRY and Lucy Lipscomb, dau. of Joseph Lipscomb. Sur. James Roseberry. Wit. Barnet Lipscomb and Moses Lipscomb. p 59

28 March 1792. Moses ROW and Rebecca Mantalowe. Sur. Abraham Estes. Married by Rev. William Douglas who says Rowe. p 58

24 September 1803. James ROWE and Jane Draper. Sur. David Draper. Married 29 September by Rev. Duke W. Hullum. p 108

14 November 1803. James ROWE and Elizabeth Rowe, of age. Sur. Hezekiah Faris. Wit. Richard Rowe. p 109

13 September 1779. Jesse ROWE and Jane Faris, dau. of
Mary Faris. Sur. Robert Mickle. p 13

10 October 1791. John ROWE and Sarah Anderson. Sur.
William Walker. p 56

6 October 1812. Zachariah ROWE and Henney Locker. Sur.
Alexander Locker. Zachariah is over 21 years of age.
p 149

11 November 1808. William RUTHERFORD and Elizabeth
Lawrence. Sur. John F. Parish. Married 22 November by
Rev. Lewis Chaudoin. p 131

26 July 1803. William RUTTER and Charlotte Inscip.
Sur. William Haywood. Wit. John W. Sale. p 107

25 November 1797. James RYAN and Jemima Harris, dau.
of Patrick Harris. Sur. Thomas Ryan. Wit. Bolden
Badget. Married by Rev. Martin Walton. p 82

13 December 1814. John RYAN and Elizabeth Badgett, dau.
of Thomas Badgett. Sur. Simon Foster. Wit. John
Badgett. Returned 17 January 1815 by Rev. William
Cooke. p 156

13 January 1798. Thomas RYAN and Peggy Ward, dau. of
William Ward. Sur. John Foster. Wit. Major Ryan.
Married 17 January by Rev. Martin Walton. p 84

14 December 1795. William RYAN and Nancy Armstrong.
Thomas Meriwether gives consent for each party. Sur.
John Tilford. Wit. Edward Garland. Married 17
December by Rev. Martin Walton. p 74

13 August 1792. Julias SANDERS and Ann Thomson. Sur.
Edward Thomson. p 58

11 February 1782. Joseph SANDIDGE and Elizabeth Wright.
Sur. James Byars. Married 14 February by Rev. William
Douglas who says Sandage. p 19

16 December 1793. Nathaniel SARGEANT and Patsey Boyd,
dau. of John Boyd. Sur. Thomas Poindexter. Wit. John
Seargeant. Married 19 December by Rev. Richard Pope.
p 64

22 December 1814. Mann SATTERWHITE and Ann Anderson,
dau. of M. Anderson. Sur. James Trice. Wit. Dorothy
Anderson and Elizabeth Trice. Mann Satterwhite is of
the City of Richmond. Married by Rev. William
Crawford, M. P. E. C. Returned 7 January 1815. p 156

8 September 1777. James SCOTT and Anna Gray. Married by Rev. William Douglas who says Scot. The Douglas Register p 18

25 October 1798. John SCUDDY and Elizabeth O. Brickley, (Betcy), of age. Sur. John Toler. Wit. William Bickley and Judeth Arnold. W. McGee, Sr. is guardian of John. Married 8 November by Rev. William Cooke who says Betsey Bickley. p 86

19 December 1812. Jasper A. SEARGEANT and Eliza Parrish, dau. of Humphrey Parrish. Sur. Nelson Parrish. Jasper is son of John Seargeant. Married 26 December by Rev. John Lasley. p 150

23 January 1788. John SEARGEANT and Frances Trice, 21 years old 15 November 1787, dau. of William and Mary Trice. Sur. George Bell. Wit. Forest Green. Married 24 January by Rev. John Lasley. p 39

10 October 1793. William SEARGEANT, Jr. and Elizabeth Purkins, dau of John Purkins. Sur. Bartlett Henson. Wit. William Seargeant. Married by Rev. Richard Pope who says Perkins. p 63

13 March 1813. William SEARGEANT and Anney Snead. Sur. William Cooper. Wit. Jesse Fulcher. Married 15 March by Rev. John Lasley who says William Seargeant, Sr. p 151

3 December 1801. John SEAY and Jane Windrow, dau. of Richard Windrow. Sur. John Windrow. Married by Rev. John Lasley. p 99

14 September 1789. Thomas SEAY and Mary Harris, dau. of Micajah Harris. Sur. John Fleming. Wit. William Spicer. Married 17 September by Rev. Charles Hopkins. p 46

20 October 1808. Charles SEXTON and Lucy Poindexter. John Poindexter gives consent for Lucy. Sur. James Gooch. Married by Rev. John Lasley. p 131

2 July 1781. John SHARP and Nancy Gentry, dau. of James Gentry. Sur. Micajah Sims. Wit. Thomas Higgason. p 17

23 August 1785. Martin SHARP and Elizabeth Hambleton, over 21 years of age, dau. of Sarah Hamilton and sister of Duke Hambleton. Sur. William Sharp. p 29

12 November 1787. Robert SHARP and Nancy Baker. Sur. Thomas Davis. p 37

10 October 1803. William SHARP, Junr. and Elizabeth
Pettit. Sur. James Sharp. Wit. Thomas Swift and Harriet
Swift. p 108

6 November 1786. David SHELTON and Henrietta Thomasson,
dau. of Samuel Thomasson. Sur. Poindexter Thomasson.
Wit. Nathaniel Thomasson and Samuel Thomasson, Jr. Married 7 November by Rev. William Douglas. p 33

5 June 1798. James SHELTON and Elizabeth Thomson, dau.
of Joseph Thomson. Sur. David Richardson. James is of
St. Martin's Parish. Elizabeth is of Fredricksville
Parish. Married 7 June by Rev. John D. Blair. p 85

20 May 1781. Samuel SHELTON and Jenny Henderson, over
21 years of age. Sur. John Nuckols. Wit. John Henderson, p 17

12 February 1782. Thomas SHELTON and Ciscely Dabney.
Sur. James Dabney. p 19

10 September 1792. Thomas SHELTON and Milley Atkinson,
dau. of Sarey Atkinson. Sur. John Austin. Wit. Samuel
Hunter. p 58

12 May 1809. Thomas SHELTON and Sally Farrar. Sur.
Matthew Farrar. p 135

10 July 1809. William SHELTON and Salley Landrum, over
21 years of age. Sur. Paul Talbot. p 136

16 July 1812. Anderson SHEPHERD and Polly Dalton, over
21 years of age. Sur. David Dalton. Married 13 August by
Rev. John Lasley. p 148

21 February 1786. Phillip SHEPHERD and Susannah Thomson.
Sur. John Thomson. Wit. Thomas Thomson. p 31

14 October 1799. David SHEPHERDSON and Oney Bibb. Sur.
Ben Bibb. p 90

15 October 1808. John SHEPHERDSON and Polly Groom, over
21 years of age. Sur. William Groom. p 131

24 December 1804. Nathan SHEPHERDSON and Nancey P.
Thomasson, over 21 years of age. Sur. John Thomasson.
Married 26 December by Rev. William Cooke. p 114

12 July 1802. Fleming SHORTT and Elizabeth Crenshaw.
Sur. Benjamin Crenshaw. p 102

2 November 1786. Thomas SHROCK and Milley Goldsmith,
dau. of William Goldsmith. Sur. William Walker. Wit.
Randolph Watson and Lucy Goldsmith. Thomas, of age, is
of Albemarle County. p 33

16 August 1788. Benjamin SIMS and Lucy Lipscomb, dau.
of Fran. Lipscomb. Sur. Anderson Peers. Wit. Micajah
Sims and John Lipscomb. p 41

1 December 1804. Benjamin SIMS and Elizabeth Boyd, dau.
of John Boyd. Sur. Thomas Boyd, brother of Elizabeth.
Married 2 December by Rev. John Lasley. p 113

13 February 1779. David SIMS, Jun. and Elizabeth Dickenson. John Dickenson is guardian of Elizabeth. Sur. John
Sanders. Wit. Watson Gentry. p 12

5 November 1799. David SIMS and Nancy Whitlock, of
lawful age. Thomas Whitlock gives consent for Nancy.
Sur. Thomas Boyd. Wit. John Whitlock. Married by
Rev. John Lasley. p 91

11 November 1803. David SIMS and Nancey Strong, dau. of
George Strong. Sur. William B. Cosby. Married 24 November by Rev. William Cooke. p 131

14 March 1808. Garland SIMS and Elizabeth Shepherdson.
Sur. John Shepherdson or Vaden Sims. p 129

9 May 1791. John SIMS, Jr. and Elizabeth Sharp Hanes,
dau. of Christopher Hanes. Sur. Asa Sims. Wit. Keziah
Hanes and John Dickason. p 54

25 September 1795. John SIMS and Elizabeth Lipscomb,
dau. of Francis Lipscomb. Sur. Micajah Sims. Wit. John
Lipscomb. Married 1 October by Rev. William Cooke. p 73

18 January 1796. John SIMS and Anna Terry. Sur. George
Byars. Married 21 January by Rev. Martin Walton. p 74

7 September 1784. Lewis SIMS and Peggy Leonard. Sur.
David Leonard. p 26

13 January 1806. Matthew SIMS and Mary Anderson, dau.
of Nathan Anderson. Sur. John Anderson. Wit. Otho
Williams. Married by Rev. John B. Magruder of the
Methodist Episcopal Church. Returned 21 March 1809.
p 119

17 June 1787. Micajah SIMS and Delphia Peers, dau. of
Thomas Peers. Sur. Lyddal Britton. Wit. Andrew Peers.
p 36

5 May 1795. Nathan SIMS and Elizabeth Barrett. Sur.
Robert Barrett. p 71

6 January 1802. Nathan SIMS and Caty Phillips. Sur.
Samuel Hill. Wit. Thomas Phillips and Elizabeth Waddy.
p 100

19 September 1800. Richard SIMS and Peggy Wright. Sur.
John Peay. Wit. Wright Bond and William Gradey. Mar-
ried by Rev. Richard Ferguson. The return is dated 19
August 1801. p 94

16 December 1815. Thomas SIMS and Jane Anderson, dau.
of Nathan Anderson, who is surety. Wit. William
Anderson. p 160

16 November 1789. Vadin SIMS and Jane Groom, above 21
years of age, dau. of William Groom. Sur. Robert
Stewart. p 47

2 October 1788. John SLADYEN and Judith Garland, dau.
of Robert Garland. Sur. Daniel Sladyen. Wit. Charles
Garland and Sarah Garland. Married 4 October by Rev.
William Douglas. p 41

2 February 1780. Charles SLAUGHTER and Elizabeth Poindexter. Sur. John Poindexter. p 14

24 March 1790. John SLAUGHTER and Ann Lewis Thomson,
dau. of Waddy Thomson. Sur. Samuel Poindexter. Married 26 March by Rev. William Douglas. p 50

30 December 1796. Arthur SLAYDEN and Lucy Green. Sur.
George Walker. Married 1 January 1797 by Rev. Richard
Pope. p 79

9 July 1804. Thomas SLEDD and Betsey Marks. Sur. John
Sledd. p 112

13 November 1809. Ambrose SMITH and Sarah Gibbens.
Thomas Gibbens, of Orange County, gives consent for
Sarah. Sur. William Patterson. p 137

7 May 1811. Ballard SMITH and _____ Price, dau. of
Major William Price. Sur. Wilson Price. p 144

11 May 1808. Barnett SMITH and Mary Grayson. Sur.
Nelson Moss. p 129

3 January 1782. Champness SMITH and Elizabeth Hubbard.
Sur. Robert Kimbrough. Married 4 January by Rev. William Douglas. p 18

17 November 1783. Charles SMITH and Nancy Johnson. Sur. James Barnett. Married 20 November by Rev. William Douglas. p 24

21 November 1786. Christopher SMITH and Mary Anderson. Sur. Robert Anderson, Jr. Married by Rev. William Douglas. p 34

5 November 1810. Dabney SMITH and Agnes Walton, under 21 years of age, dau. of Joel Walton. Sur. William Walton. Married 8 November by Rev. William Cooke. p 141

12 January 1788. David SMITH and Frances Dickason, dau. of Robert Dickason. Sur. Fleming Thomason. Wit. Jonathan Dickason and James Dickason. p 39

13 July 1815. David SMITH and Frances Lipscomb. Sur. William Dickinson. Wit. Christopher Smith and Oliver Smith. Married by Rev. William Y. Hiter. p 158

18 February 1811. Ezekiel SMITH and Mildred Grimstead, under 21 years of age. Sur. David Grimstead. Married 21 February by Rev. John Lasley. p 143

27 December 1804. George SMITH and Elizabeth Waddy, over 21 years of age. Sur. Samuel Waddy, Jr. Married by Rev. William Cooke. p 114

2 July 1810. Jaariorigim SMITH and Mary C. Dickinson, dau. of Charles Dickinson. Sur. Dickerson Morris. p 140

13 November 1786. John SMITH and Frances Terry, 21 years of age. Sur. John Lipscomb. John is son of John Smith. p 34

27 March 1791. John SMITH and Elizabeth Timberlake. Sur. Joel Timberlake. Returned 29 April by Rev. John Lasley. p 54

22 December 1807. John SMITH and Elizabeth Swift, under 21 years of age, dau. of Richard Swift. Sur. Elisha Smith. p 127

7 January 1789. Joseph SMITH and Elizabeth Edwards. Sur. Richard Jones. Married 8 January by Rev. William Douglas. p 43

6 October 1800. Leven SMITH and Nancey Desper. Sur. Zachariah Pulliam. Wit. William Boyd. Married 7 October by Rev. John Lasley. p 95

10 November 1794. Nathan SMITH and Barbara Terry, of age, dau. of Henrietta Terry. Sur. Thomas Smith. Wit. William Terry and Sarah Terry. Married 27 November by Rev. William Cooke. p 69

17 May 1811. Nathaniel A. SMITH and Lavinia Callis, under 21 years of age, dau. of W. O. Callis. Sur. William Barrett. p 144

10 December 1792. Reubin SMITH and Elizabeth Duke, 21 years of age. Sur. Richard K. Tyler. Wit. William Smith, Ann Smith, George Smith, Jr. and George Smith, Sr. p 60

8 July 1780. Robert SMITH and Susannah Woodrum. Married by Rev. William Douglas. The Douglas Register p 20

10 September 1787. Rodes SMITH and Unity Thomson. Sur. Asa Thomson. Married by Rev. William Douglas. p 36

24 March 1788. Skelton SMITH and Dianah Moss, dau. of John Moss. Sur. Joseph Kimbrough. Wit. John Kimbrough and William Kimbrough. Married 3 April by Rev. William Douglas. p 40

11 November 1799. Skelton SMITH and Jane Cosby Yancey. Sur. W. Cooke. Wit. Rev. John Poindexter. Married 21 November by Rev. William Cooke. p 91

8 December 1788. Thomas SMITH and Elizabeth Terry. Henirita Terry gives consent for Elizabeth. Sur. William Nuckolls. Wit. William Gibson. p 42

19 December 1768 William SMITH and Elizabeth Young. John Fox gives consent for Elizabeth. Sur. Thomas Ballard Smith. Wit. Caty Smith, John Nelson and Ann Smith. p 1

6 October 1789. William SMITH and Anne Byars. John Crawford is Anne's guardian. Sur. John Lea. Wit. James Crawford and Joel Cook. William is son of Edward Smith. Married 8 October by Rev. John Lasley. p 46

7 January 1797. Captain William SMITH and Ann Bibb. Sur. Nathaniel Garland. Wit. Wingfield Cosby. p 80

1 September 1800. William SMITH and Nancey Smith. Sur. Thomas Smith. Married 3 September by Rev. John Lasley. p 94

14 January 1811. William SNEAD and Patsy Ware. Sur. William Walton. Married by Rev. William Cooke. p 143

13 May 1793. Bartelette SNELSON and Elizabeth Luck,
dau. of Elizabeth Dickenson. Sur. George Wilkerson.
Wit. Garland Dickenson. p 62

19 January 1813. John SNELSON and Jemima Armstrong,
dau. of William Armstrong. Sur. John Armstrong. Wit.
John Armstrong, Sr. p 150

29 January 1786. Nathaniel SNELSON and Sally Spicer.
Married by Rev. John Waller. Ministers' Returns p 360

15 January 1812. William SOUTHWORTH and Sarah Jennings,
(Sally), dau. of Thomas Jennings. Sur. Charles Carter
Jennings. p 146

7 November 1787. Edward SPENCER and Eleanor Woolfolk,
of Orange County. Edward Spencer is of Orange County.
Married by Rev. John Lasley. Ministers' Returns p 361

21 November 1796. Benjamin SPICER and Elizabeth Fleming,
21 years of age, dau. of William Fleming, deceased. Sur.
John Fleming, her brother. Wit. George Lumsden. Married
24 November by Rev. William Cooke. p 78

22 December 1794. Rosser SPICER and Sarah Newton, dau.
of Samuel Newton. Sur. William Spicer. Wit. James
Seay and John Davis. Married 26 December by Rev.
William Cooke. p 70

11 April 1789. William SPICER and Sarah Harris, dau.
of Micajah Harris. Sur. James Poindexter. Wit. Peter
Smith and William McGehee. Married 16 April by Rev.
Charles Hopkins. p 45

13 November 1789. Jeremiah SPROUSE and Elizabeth
Depriest. Sur. William Gibson. Jeremiah's father
gave consent but his name was omitted. p 47

22 July 1784. Maddox STANLEY and Sarah Bunch. Married
by Rev. William Douglas. The Douglas Register p 23

8 September 1802. Strangeman STANLEY and Patsey Watkins,
dau. of Benjamin Watkins. Sur. Jehu Walton. Wit.
George Gentry and Absolum Hall. Married 9 September by
Rev. William Cooke. p 102

14 October 1793. William STEELE and Mary Jackson.
Sur. Nelson Anderson. Married by Rev. Martin Walton
who says Polley. p 63

27 June 1799. Julius STEPHENS and Fanny Trainum, 21
years of age, dau. of Jaconias Trainum. Sur. Jack
Trainum. Wit. Frederick Harris, Jr. Married 27 July
by Rev. William Cooke who says Trainham. p 89

13 September 1781. Charles STEWARD, Junr. and Mildred Stuart. Sur. Charles Steward, Senr. (This name, for both father and son, is also written Stuart on the bond). Married 14 September by Rev. William Douglas who says Stewart for each party. p 18

14 January 1811. John STEWART and Mary Gooch. Sur. Rowland Gooch, Jr. p 143

25 April 1801. James STODGEL and Polley Diggs. Sur. Thomas Diggs. Married 28 April by Rev. William Baskett. p 98

9 July 1799. James STOGEL and Dicey Ascue. Married by Rev. William Baskett. Ministers' Returns p 372

20 June 1812. Thomas J. STONE and Salley L. Cawthon. Married by Rev. John Lasley. Ministers' Returns p 388

4 September 1769. Joseph STREET and Sarah Tait. Sur. Samuel Waddy. Wit. Mary Burnett and Sarah Waddy. p 2

15 February 1785. John STRINGER and Henrietta Foster. Sur. Edmond Foster. p 28

15 August 1792. George STRONG and Charity Hickason, daughter-in-law of Mark Wheeler. Sur. George Harris. Wit. Richard Higgason and John Strong. p 58

8 January 1798. Thomas STUBBS and Salley Harris. Sur. William Cooke. Married 11 January by Rev. William Cooke. p 83

26 April 1811. Archibald SWIFT and Sally Parsons. Samuel Parsons gives consent for Sally. Sur. Pleasant Hanes. Wit. Charles Swift. p 144

31 January 1783. John SWIFT and Ann Swift, (Nancy), dau. of Richard Swift. Sur. William Swift. Wit. David Anderson. p 22

6 February 1783. John SWIFT and Sarah Swift. Married by Rev. William Douglas. The Douglas Register p 22

22 July 1805. John SWIFT and Polly Anthony, over 21 years of age. James and Mary Anthony give consent for Polly. Sur. James Gooch. Wit. Daniel Gardner. Married by Rev. William Cooke. p 116

10 September 1784. Lewis SYMES and Peggie Leonard. Married by Rev. William Douglas. The Douglas Register p 23

23 December 1779. William TAITE and Margaret Taite. Sur. Enos Tait. p 13

26 March 1804. William TALIAFERRO and Mary Anderson.
Sur. Reubin Reynolds. Married by Rev. Samuel Monett.
p 112

24 December 1793. George TALLEY and Salley Cole, dau.
of William Cole. Sur. William Gibson. Wit. William
Talley, Lydia Talley and Thomas Knighton. Married 26
December by Rev. William Douglas. p 65

13 December 1793. Michael TALLEY and Barbara Cole.
Sur. Samuel Cole. Married by Rev. William Douglas. p 64

13 September 1813. Nathaniel TALLEY and Sarah Thomason,
dau. of Fleming Thomasson who is surety. Wit. Pollard
Smith Thomasson. Married 2 October by Rev. William
Cooke. p 153

17 May 1791. Story TALLEY and Elizabeth Trainom, dau.
of Charles Trainom. Sur. John Harger. Wit. John
Fretwell. p 54

__ February 1791. William TALLEY and Lidia Cole. Sur.
James Poindexter. Married __ March by Rev. William
Douglas. p 53

7 October 1773. Reuben TALLY and Martha Dyer. Married
by Rev. William Douglas. The Douglas Register p 14

9 December 1805. Mills TANDY and Amelia Wash, dau. of
William Graves. Sur. George Wash. Mills Tandy is of
Orange County. (See Mills Tandy). p 118

17 December 1805. Mills TANDY and Amelia Graves. Married by Rev. William Cooke. (See Mills Tandy).
Ministers' Returns p 381

14 March 1808. Ralph TANDY and Mitilda McGehee, dau.
of Edward McGehee. Sur. Mordecai Cooke. Wit. Oswell
McGehee. Married 23 March by Rev. William Cooke who
says Matilda. p 129

16 February 1808. Nathaniel TARBET and Susannah P.
Smith, dau. of William Smith. Sur. H. Laurence. Married 18 February by Rev. William Cooke. p 128

29 December 1807. Benjamin TATE and Mary Syms. Sur.
Benjamin Sims. Married 31 December by Rev. John Lasley
who says Polley Sims. p 127

9 September 1772. Enos TATE and Elizabeth Tate, under
21 years of age, dau. of James Tate. Sur. Uriah Tate.
Wit. Robert Tate. p 5

12 March 1799. John TATE and Sally Poindexter, dau. of
William Poindexter. Sur. Benjamin Bibb. p 88

19 November 1805. John TATE and Mildred Corthan. Sur.
John Walton. Wit. David Sims, Nathaniel Tate and Molly
Sims. Married 20 November by Rev. William Cooke. p 117

12 May 1800. Joshua TATE and Salley Yancey, dau. of
Salley Yancey. Sur. Augustus Yancey. Married by Rev.
Richard Ferguson. p 93

8 October 1788. Nathan TATE and Frances Gentry, dau. of
George Gentry. Sur. John Kersey. Wit. Jesse Payne and
Nancey Gentry. p 41

13 May 1786. Nathaniel TATE and Cisiah Ward, dau. of
William Ward. Sur. Storey Talley. Wit. Joseph Suther-
land and Clevears Duke. p 32

21 December 1780. Robert TATE and Susanna Bibb. Married by Rev. William Douglas. The Douglas Register p 20

19 October 1793. Thomas TATE and Permelia Yarbrough.
Sur. John Gunter. p 63

12 October 1772. Uriah TATE and Elizabeth Graves, dau.
of Rice Graves. Sur. Enos Tate. Wit. Richard Graves
and Robert Tate. p 6

25 December 1779. William TATE and Margaret Tate. Married by Rev. William Douglas. The Douglas Register p 19

26 September 1770. James TAYLOR and Mary Moorman, dau.
of Charles Moorman. Sur. John Bunch. Wit. Nathaniel
Anderson and Elizabeth Anderson. Col. Pendleton and
Capt. James Taylor are guardians of James Taylor. p 3

6 June 1772. James TAYLOR and Elizabeth Bark. Sur.
Walter Goldsmith. Wit. Henry Garrett and George Pottie.
p 5

17 July 1796. William TAYLOR and Fanny Foster, dau. of
William Foster. Sur. Nelson Foster. Married by Rev.
John Lasley. p 77

6 December 1780. John TELFORD and Margaret King. Married by Rev. William Douglas. The Douglas Register p 20

25 November 1780. Joel TERRELL and Lucy Ragland, under
21 years of age, dau. of Samuel Ragland. Sur. Charles
Wingfield. Wit. Susannah Ragland and Ann Jones. p 16

28 November 1805. Lynch TERRELL and Ellenor A. Callis,
dau. of W. O. Callis. Sur. Richard Tyler. Wit. William
O. Barrett and Cleon M. Callis. p 117

8 April 1782. Richmond TERRELL and Cissilla Darricott.
Sur. William Terrell. Married 25 April by Rev. William
Douglas who says Cecelia. p 20

24 November 1813. Richmond TERRELL and Sarah M. Overton,
dau. of John Overton. Sur. Elijah Hutchinson. Wit. Eliza
Bacon and John T. Fleming. Sarah's name is also written
Sarah G. Overton on the bond. p 154

20 October 1780. Thomas TERRELL and Sarah Shelton, dau.
of David Shelton. Sur. George Lumsden. Wit. John Gunnell and Joseph Shelton. Thomas is son of William
Terrell. Married 30 October by Rev. William Douglas.
p 15

14 April 1812. Champ TERRY and Nancey Dunn. Sur. William Terry. Married by Rev. John Lasley. p 147

9 October 1784. Emanuel TERRY and Elizabeth Thomson,
21 years of age, dau. of John Thomson. Sur. John Tins-
dale. Married 14 October by Rev. William Douglas. p 26

25 January 1790. James TERRY and Anna Smith, dau. of
John Smith, D. S. Sur. Thomas Smith. Wit. James
Byars and Nathan Smith. p 49

18 March 1797. Joseph TERRY and Polly Smith, dau. of
John Smith, D. S. Wit. William Gibson. Married 23
March by Rev. William Cooke. p 81

14 December 1782. Stephen TERRY and Mildred Bagby, dau.
of John Bagby. Sur. William Bagby. Wit. Garland Cosby.
p 21

14 December 1793. Stephen TERRY and Sarah Davis, over
21 years of age. Sur. John Bagby. Wit. Henry Garrett.
p 64

27 November 1811. Stephen TERRY and Rhoda Gooch, dau.
of John Gooch. Sur. Gideon Gooch. Wit. James Terry.
p 145

11 June 1794. William TERRY and Sarah Crank, dau. of
George Crank. Sur. John Smith. Wit. Nathan Smith.
Married 15 June by Rev. William Cooke. p 67

15 March 1804. William TERRY and Elizabeth Gooch, dau.
of John Gooch. Sur. William Gooch. p 111

17 December 1806. William M. TERRY and Elizabeth Crank.
David Hall is Elizabeth's guardian. Sur. John Waller.
Wit. William Smith, Dr. p 123

10 January 1799. Anderson THACKER and Sary Martin, of
lawful age. Sary resides with Isaac Thacker. Sur.
George Green. Married 11 January by Rev. Richard Pope
who says Sarah. p 87

31 July 1781. Archelaus THACKER and Ann Chace. Married
by Rev. William Douglas. The Douglas Register p 21

30 January 1805. Benjamin THACKER and Nancey Clarke,
dau. of Francis Clarke and sister of Edmund Clarke who
is surety. Wit. Samuel Clarke and Caleb Clarke. Benjamin is of Goochland County. Married 31 January by Rev.
William Baskett. p 115

25 October 1786. Daniel THACKER and Lucy Humphrey, 21
years of age. Sur. Benjamin Thacker. Wit. Atha^s. Barnett.
p 33

6 October 1800. Isaac THACKER, Junr. and Rishey Morgan.
Sur. Overton Lowry. Wit. Ann Thacker. Married 8 October by Rev. Richard Pope. p 95

_____ 1814. John THACKER and Betsey Lewis. Married
by Rev. William Y. Hiter. Ministers' Returns p 390

17 February 1814. John THACKER and Elizabeth Ailstock,
over 21 years of age. Sur. William Ailstock. p 155

11 July 1786. Reuben THACKER and Jane Ward. William
Ward gives consent for Jane. Sur. John Ward. Wit.
Thomas Gardner and Nath'l Tate. p 32

3 December 1784. William THACKER and Elizabeth Smith.
Married by Rev. William Douglas. The Douglas Register
p 23

5 December 1812. Archibald THOMAS and Salley Seay. Sur.
Thomas Seay. Married 10 December by Rev. William Cooke.
p 149

24 January 1786. Charles THOMAS and Sally Adams, dau.
of George Adams. Sur. Thomas Woodger. Wit. Wilson
Adams and Edward Dyhouse. p 31

26 July 1808. James THOMAS and Elizabeth Waldrope. Sur.
James Matthews. Wit. Samuel Waldrope. p 130

4 October 1796. John THOMAS and Meredith Christmas,
(Peggy), dau. of Thomas Christmas. Sur. Thomas Gardner. Married 6 October by Rev. Martin Walton. p 78

13 October 1797. William THOMAS and Patsy Woodall.
Sur. Charles Woodall. Married 17 October by Rev. William Baskett. p 82

10 September 1812. Wright THOMAS and Polly Hatton.
Sur. George Carnall. Wit. Henry Chiles. Married by
Rev. John Lasley. p 148

15 April 1784. Byars THOMASON and Sarah White. Sur.
John White, Junr. Married by Rev. William Douglas. p 25

21 December 1780. John THOMASON and Frances Cook, 21
years of age, sister of W___ Cooke. Sur. Samuel
Thomasson. Wit. Martha Day and Ann Harris. Married 23
December by Rev. William Douglas. p 16

23 April 1786. Richard THOMASON and Sarah Terry. Sur.
Samuel Thomasson. Wit. Stephen Terry and Henrietta
Terry. Married 25 April by Rev. William Douglas who
says: "both of Louisa (18 miles)". p 32

28 July 1774. Elias THOMASSON and Mary Harris. Sur.
Samuel Thomasson. p 8

22 December 1812. Elias THOMASSON and Susannah Harris.
Sur. John P. Thomasson. Married 24 December by Rev.
William Cooke. p 150

24 October 1814. George THOMASSON and Dianah Lipscomb.
Sur. John Beadles. Wit. William W. Beadles. Married
by Rev. William Y. Hiter. p 156

6 May 1799. John THOMASSON and Elizabeth Nuckolds.
Sur. Billey Snead. Married 8 May by Rev. William
Cooke. p 89

20 September 1806. John THOMASSON, Jr. and Nancey
Hancock, over 21 years of age. Sur. John Thomasson, Sr.
Wit. Nathan Shepheardson. p 122

18 December 1773. Nathaniel THOMASSON and Martha Wood.
Sur. Samuel Thomasson and David Wood. p 8

13 December 1783. Samuel THOMASSON. Junr. and Liddia
McGehee, dau of William McGehee. Sur. Samuel Thomasson, Sr. Married 14 December. No Minister's name is
given. p 24

17 April 1786. William THOMASSON and Unity Hix. Sur.
Samuel Thomason. Married 18 April by Rev. William
Douglas who says: "both of Louisa ___ 4 miles". p 32

27 November 1779. David THOMPSON and Eleanor Thomson.
Sur. Anthony Thomson. David is son of Waddy Thomson.
On the bond his name is also written David Thomson. Married 30 November by Rev. William Douglas. p 13

18 November 1805. John THOMPSON and Polly Gooch. Sur.
Stephen Gooch. Married by Rev. Richard Ferguson. p 117

19 November 1799. Richard THOMPSON and Mary McGehee.
Married by Rev. Richard Ferguson. Ministers' Returns
p 373

26 May 1794. William THOMPSON and Fanny Parish. Sur.
Joel Parish. p 67

24 May 1785. Anderson THOMSON and Ann Clopton Anderson,
dau. of Nelson Anderson. Sur. Asa Sims. p 28

19 November 1778. Charles THOMSON and Anne Jerdone, dau.
of Sarah Jerdone. Sur. John Nelson. Wit. George Pottie
and Elizabeth Jerdone. p 11

14 December 1800. Charles THOMSON and Nancy Graves, dau.
of William Graves. Sur. William Kennedy. p 96

22 February 1788. Clifton THOMSON and Mary Ragland.
Samuel Ragland is Mary's guardian. Sur. William Thomson.
Wit. Sarah Meriwether, Nicholas Meriwether, Richard Johnson and W. Cooke. Married 26 February by Rev. William
Douglas. p 39

30 June 1786. David THOMSON and Anna Cory, widow. Sur.
James Bibb. p 32

15 March 1785. Edmond THOMSON and Ann Anderson, dau.
of Michael Anderson. Sur. Edmond Anderson. Wit. Thomas
Anderson. p 28

7 November 1810. Garland THOMSON and Sarah J. Mitchell,
dau. of Thomas Mitchell. Sur. William Mitchell, Jr.
Wit. T. H. Mitchell, Jr. p 141

8 February 1803. Glover THOMSON and Betsey Edwards. Sur.
John Hill. Wit. Salley Gooch. p 105

6 July 1783. James THOMSON and Tempe Mooney. Married
by Rev. William Douglas. The Douglas Register p 23

28 March 1789. John THOMSON and Sarah Ragland, (Salley),
granddaughter of Samuel Ragland who is her guardian.
Sur. Clifton Thomson. Wit. Elizabeth Ragland and Samuel
Bickley. Married 31 March by Rev. William Douglas. p 44

13 December 1806. John THOMSON and Milly Hansford, over 21 years of age. Sur. Samuel Wharton. p 122

3 January 1790. Lewis THOMSON and Nancy Thomas. Sur. William Thomason. p 48

11 January 1790. Robert THOMSON and Mary Anderson, dau. of Matthew Anderson who is surety. Wit. Anthony Thomson and Elizabeth Anderson. p 48

16 December 1794. Samuel THOMSON and Nancy Cole, dau. of William Cole who is surety. Wit. William Cole, Jr. and Thomas Knighton. p 69

7 August 1787. Waddy THOMSON and Elizabeth Anderson, dau. of Richard Anderson. Sur. Thomas Bell. Wit. A. Thomson. Married 8 August by Rev. William Douglas. p 36

11 October 1802, William THOMSON and Elizabeth Tally. Sur, Claybourn Gooch. Married 12 October by Rev. Duke W. Hullam. p 102

27 April 1812. Reubin THORNTON and Maria T. Winston. Peter Dudley is Maria's guardian. Sur. Thomas Johnson, Jr. Married 30 April by Rev. William Cooke. p 147

5 September 1803. Matthew THURSTON and Polley Glenn. Sur. John Glenn. Married 15 September by Rev. Lewis Chaudoin who says Matthew is of Goochland County. p 107

5 December 1780. John TILFORD and Margaret King. Sur. Thomas King. p 16

24 December 1793. Daniel TILLER and Agnes Matthews, 21 years old and upward. Sur. Samuel Harris. Wit. Solomon Edwards. Married 25 December by Rev. Martin Walton. p 65

14 March 1814. Joel TIMBERLAKE and Sarah Thompson. Sur, Joel Timberlake. Married 17 March by Rev. Claibourne Walton. p 155

12 April 1773 John TIMBERLAKE and Christiana Thomason, dau. of George Thomason who is surety, p 6

13 March 1809. John TIMBERLAKE and Margaret Allen. Sur. Reuben Cowherd. p 134

14 January 1805. David TISDALE and Elizabeth Y. Young. Sur, Isaac Morris. p 144

16 December 1802. James TISDALE and Fanny Lipscomb, of age. Sur. Tandy Lipscomb. Wit. Nancy Lipscomb and Patsey Lipscomb. p 104

15 December 1809. John TISDALE and Frances Johnson, over 21 years of age. Sur. Nuckolds Johnson. Married 18 December by Rev. John Lasley. p 137

14 January 1799. Robert TISDALE and Sally Beadles. Sur. James Beadles. p 88

24 December 1770. Shirley TISDALE and Ursula Ragland. Sur. Samuel Morris. Wit. George Terrell. p 4

5 August 1800. Terrell TISDALE and Susanna Parrish. Sur. Joel Parrish. p 94

20 November 1793. William TISDALE and Polley Morris. San Morris gives consent for Polley. Sur. Shirley Tisdale. Wit. Henry Tisdale. Married 21 November by Rev. Richard Pope. p 63

24 May 1785. Dr. Andrew TODD and Mary Todd, dau. of John Todd. Sur. Richard Paulett. Wit. Elizabeth McCalla. p 29

31 December 1781. Robert TODD and Anne Todd. Sur. John Parker. p 18

9 August 1803. Paul TOLBERT and Betsy Landrum, dau. of Francis Landrum. Sur. John Landrum. Married by Rev. Duke W. Hullam. p 107

12 January 1789. Adam TOLER and Mary Pottie. Sur. Archibald Dick. Married 14 January by Rev. Charles Hopkins. p 43

25 October 1797. Jesse TOLER and Polley Toler. Sur. John Toler. Married 26 October by Rev. William Cooke. p 82

12 October 1807. William F. TOLER and Polly Walton Smith, 21 years of age. Sur. George Harris. Wit. William Smith, Dr. and W. Cooke. Married 13 October by Rev. William Cooke. p 126

25 December 1786. William TOMPKINS and Mary Mickie. Henry A. Johnson is guardian of Mary. Sur. John Mickie. Wit. William Piers. Married 26 December by Rev. William Douglas. p 34

2 December 1811. Jechonias TRAINHAM and Martha Grubbs. Sur. George Strong. Wit. Charity Strong. Married 4 December by Rev. William Cooke. p 145

3 February 1809. Samuel TRAINHAM and Sarah Durvin.
Sur. Absolum Hall. Wit. Thos. Holloday, William Cooke
and Anderson B. Cooke. p 133

1 September 1788. David TRAINUM and Mary Woolliams.
Sur. John Woolliams. p 41

5 November 1790. Lewis TRAINUM and Theodosia Wollowms.
(Theodosia Woollams is also on the bond). She is dau.
of John Wollowms. Sur. David Trainum. Wit. John
Smith. p 52

6 February 1808. James TRANHAM and Sarah Darvin. Sur.
Absalem Hall. Wit. Hopeful Toler. p 128

13 June 1806. Foster TRANUM and Patsey Fleming, dau.
of Ann Fleming and granddaughter of Mary Luck. Sur.
William Fleming. p 121

18 October 1800. John TRANUM and Susanna Gibson. Sur.
Dabney Gibson. Wit. Christopher Cammack, Thomas Gard-
ner and Theodosha Gibson. Married 22 October by Rev.
William Cooke who says Trainham. p 95

20 December 1805. Anderson TRICE and Martha Sandidge,
dau. of Joseph Sandidge. Sur. James Trice. Wit. Lucy
Minor. Married by Rev. Richard Ferguson. p 118

16 August 1796. Dabney TRICE and Fanny Lipscomb. Sur.
John Lipscomb. p 77

11 February 1809. Dabney TRICE and Unity Smith Thomason,
dau. of Unity Thomason who is her guardian. Sur. Aaron
Arnold. p 134

21 February 1787. James TRICE and Polly Smith, dau. of
Nathan Smith. Sur. John Trice. Wit. James Poindexter.
Married 22 February by Rev. William Douglas. p 35

21 August 1794. James TRICE and Elizabeth Anderson, dau.
of Nor M. Anderson. Sur. Randolph Perry. Wit. Richard
Anderson. p 67

9 September 1783. John TRICE and Patty Smith. Sur.
Nathan Smith. Married by Rev. William Douglas. p 23

9 May 1786. William TRICE and Mary Watkins. Sur. Isham
Watkins. (See William Trise). p 31

16 August 1790. William TRICE, Jr. and Ann Nelson.
Sur. James Trice. Married by Rev. William Douglas.
p 50

8 March 1814. William TRICE and Elizabeth Wallace.
Sur. John Day. p 155

19 May 1784. William TRISE and Mary Watkins. Married
by Rev. David Thomson. (See William Trice). Ministers'
Returns p 360

7 October 1783. Samuel TROTMAN and Catherine Barnet.
Married by Rev. William Douglas. The Douglas Register
p 23

9 July 1798. Henry TROWER and Martha Anderson. Sur.
Charles Anderson. p 85

8 August 1791. John TROWER and Mary Bellomy, over 21
years of age, dau. of John Bellomy. Sur. John R. Ragland. Wit. Thomas Johnson, Minister. p 55

12 March 1804. Solomon TROWER and Mary Anderson, of
age. Sur. John Trower. p 111

7 January 1801. George W. TRUEHEART and Fanny G. Overton.
John Overton gives consent for Fanny. Sur. William B.
Winston. Wit. Peggey Bickley. p 97

_____ 1798. Hardin TURNER and Patsy Crenshaw.
Sur. John Fretwell. Married 21 December by Rev.
Reuben Ford. p 83

27 February 1792. James TURNER and Mary Gooch. Sur.
John Fleeman. p 58

11 August 1789. John TURNER and Sarah Carpenter. Sur.
John Carpenter. Married 13 August by Rev. John Waller.
p 45

7 April 1798. Thomas TURNER and Unity Smith. Sur.
Nathan Smith. p 84

19 December 1802. David TYLER and Mary Bunch, dau. of
Mary Bunch. Sur. Nathaniel Bunch. Wit. John Boyd.
Married by Rev. John Lasley. p 104

6 August 1798. John TYLER and Mildred Stone, dau. of
Stephen Stone. Sur. Lewis Johnson. Wit. Thomas Gardner. Married 7 August by Rev. Martin Walton. p 85

6 August 1800. Samuel TYREE and Nancy Cooper. Sur.
Duncan Hoomes. Samuel Tyree is of Orange County. p 94

12 April 1813. Joseph C. VALENTINE and Judith McGehee.
Sur. William McGehee. Wit. James Poindexter. Married
15 April by Rev. William Cooke. p 152

28 December 1780. Philip Vincent VASS and Susannah Mead.
Sur. Richard Sandidge. Wit. Price Vass, Rachel Vass,
Mary Vass, William Mead, Jonathan Gordon and Minor Mead.
Philip, under age, is son of Mary Vass. p 16

13 October 1813. George VEST and Susan B. Wood. Sur.
James Wood. Wit. Ann L. Wood. Married 14 October by
Rev. William Cooke. p 153

18 July 1801. Reubin VEST and Salley Lipscomb. Sur.
John Lipscomb. Married 29 July by Rev. John Lasley
who says Reuben Vest. p 98

10 June 1799. Anthony WADDY and Elizabeth Smith. Sur.
William Smith. p 89

28 April 1770. John WADDY and Jane Cobbs. Sur. Waddy
Thomson. p 2

6 March 1788. John WADDY and Mary Waddy, dau. of
Samuel Waddy. Sur. William Phillips. Wit. John
Bickley. p 39

21 October 1803. Samuel WADDY, Jr. and Patsey Homes
Kimbrough, dau. of Robert Kimbrough. Sur. William
Garrett. Wit. William Smith, B. Married by Rev.
Richard Ferguson. Returned 1 May 1804. p 108

24 July 1807. Francis WALDROPE and Susanna S. Johnson.
Sur. William Johnson. Wit. Joseph F. Johnson. p 125

31 December 1798. John WALDROPE and Mary Broaton.
Sur. William Waldrope. Wit. Elizabeth Waldrope. Married 1 January 1799 by Rev. Martin Walton. p 87

14 December 1812. Samuel WALDROPE and Judith Lipscomb.
Judith received her legacy 12 months ago from her
guardian, Benjamin Sims. Sur. Francis Waldrope. Married 15 December by Rev. William Cooke. p 150

22 August 1801. Thomas WALDROPE and Frankey Smith, dau.
of William Smith. Sur. Dabney Smith. Wit. Susanna
Smith. Married 1 September by Rev. William Cooke who
says Frances. p 99

26 December 1793. William WALDROPE and Elizabeth Ward,
dau. of William Ward. Sur. Thomas Gardner. Wit. W.(?)
Gardner, Jemima Gardner and John Ward. Married 2 January, 1794 by Rev. Martin Walton. p 65

4 November 1802. Alexander WALKER and Susanna _____.
Richard Johnson gives consent for each party. Sur.
Peter R. Johnson. p 103

14 December 1807. Joel WALKER and Polly Isbell. Sur. Joseph Isbell. p 126

13 June 1791. John WALKER and Ann Rogers. Sur. Micajah Parish. p 54

10 December 1810. Thomas WALKER and Nancy Martin. Each is over 21 years of age. Sur. Peter Stopes. p 142

2 April 1796. William WALKER and Milly Anderson. Sur. David G. Jones. Married 5 April by Rev. John Lasley. p 76

4 April 1800. William WALKER and Jane Burton. Sur. Edward Burton. Married by Rev. Hugh French. p 93

26 October 1813. William WALKER, Jr. and Elizabeth Bunch, over 21 years of age, dau. of James Bunch who is surety. p 153

26 November 1812. John WALLER and Mary H. Whitton, over 21 years of age, dau. of Mary Whitton. Sur. William Whitton. p 149

23 December 1809. Lewis F. WALLER and Jane Freeman. Sur. Thomas Woodger. Wit. William Peers. Married by Rev. Leonard Page. Returned 12 April 1810. p 138

8 August 1814. William WALLER and Sarah Hall. Sur. Nicholas Gentry. Married 11 August by Rev. Claibourne Walton. p 155

14 March 1796. Claibourn WALTON and Milly Warren. Sur. Bartholomew Warren. p 75

13 June 1791. Edward WALTON and Nancey Gentry. Sur. George Gentry. p 54

17 June 1812. Garland WALTON and Mary O. Sharp, under 21 years of age, dau. of Robert Sharp. Sur. William T. Sims. p 148

4 June 1812. Joel WALTON and Nancey Mallory. Sur. William Mallory. p 148

10 December 1792. John WALTON and Nancey Smith. Sur. William Smith. Married 13 December by Rev. Martin Walton. p 60

15 April 1788. Martin WALTON and Elizabeth Johnson. Sur. Christopher Johnson. Married by Rev. Reuben Ford. p 40

4 June 1799. Meredith WALTON and Anne Sharp, dau. of
William Sharp. Sur. Robert Sharp. Wit. William Sharp,
Jr. and Nelson Walton. Meredith Walton is of Robertson
County, Tennessee. Returned 10 August by Rev. Martin
Walton. p 89

21 March 1782. Newil WALTON and Agnes Woolfolk. Sur.
William Baker. Wit. Isham Watkins, Joseph Woolfolk and
David Hall. John Walton is guardian of Newil. p 19

29 September 1802. Robert J. WALTON and Polley Baker,Jr.,
(Mary), of age, dau of William Baker. Sur. Garland Walton. Wit. Newel Baker. p 102

31 December 1802. William WALTON and Patsy Warren.
Sur. Bartholomew Warren. p 104

14 September 1812. William WALTON and Susanna P. Wash.
Sur. Edmund Wash. Married 16 September by Rev. William
Cooke. p 148

18 March 1783. John WARD and Sarah Hambleton. Sur.
Hickason Cosby. Wit. John Peay. p 22

4 November 1786. John WARD and Savary Harris. Sur.
David Stuart. Wit. David Hambleton. p 33

7 January 1806. John WARD and Nancey Lefaun, sister of
William Lefaun who makes affadavit Nancy is 21 years of
age. Sur. John Armstrong. Wit. William Lefaun. Married 8 January by Rev. William Cooke. p 119

20 January 1806. Dudley WARE and Elizabeth Harris.
Sur. Edward Harris. Married by Rev. Richard Ferguson.
p 119

30 December 1803. Wilson WARE and Permelia Gunter,
dau. of John and Susan Gunter. Sur. Thomas Gunter.
Married by Rev. Richard Ferguson. Returned 1 May
1804. p 110

18 October 1806. Edward WARREN and Elizabeth Roberts.
Sur. Richard Roberts. p 122

14 March 1809. Dickerson WASH and Delphia Cannaday.
This name is also written Delphy Kennedy on the bond.
Sur. William Eddes. Married 15 March by Rev. John
Lasley who says Delphia Kennedy. p 135

14 September 1812. Edmund WASH and Nancy Snelson. Sur.
William Walton. Married 15 September by Rev. William
Cooke. p 149

2 February 1804. George WASH and Mary Graves, of age, dau. of William Graves. Sur. Charles Thompson, Jr. Married 14 February by Rev. William Cooke. p 111

27 January 1805. James WASH and Milley Graves, dau. of William B. Graves. Sur. Martin Wash. Wit. Harrison Graves. Married 28 January by Rev. John Lasley. p 115

3 February 1806. Martin WASH and Sally Perkins, dau. of Joseph Perkins. Sur. William Perkins. Married 6 February by Rev. John Lasley. p 120

12 April 1784. Thomas WASH and Henley Wash. Sur. Thomas Davis. p 25

3 January 1785. Thomas WASH and Susanna Fox, dau. of J. Fox. Sur. John Mickie. Wit. John Sanders and John Jackson. p 27

8 December 1794. Humphrey WATKINS and Nancy Harper. Sur, Malcolm Hart. Married by Rev. H. Goodloe. p 69

19 September 1781. Joel WATKINS and Barbary Overton Harris. Sur. Archelaus Harris. p 18

12 July 1796. Joel WATKINS and Elizabeth Thomasson. Sur. Fleming Thomasson. Wit. Joseph Bullock. p 77

13 December 1808. John WATKINS and Poley Lipscomb. Sur. William Biggers. Wit. Hopeful Toler. p 132

18 September 1809. Joseph WATKINS and Salley Gardner, over 21 years of age. Sur. Reuben Gardner. Wit. Elizabeth Gardner. p 136

4 January 1804. Stephen WATKINS and Elizabeth Hughson, dau. of John Hughson. Sur. James Hughson. Wit. Elisha Wattkins. Married 11 January by Rev. John Lasley. p 110

11 May 1795. Thomas B. WATKINS and Nancey Ragland. Sur. Samuel Ballinger. Wit. Polly Ragland. p 71

14 February 1801. David WATSON and Sarah Minor. Sur. David Yancey. p 97

28 November 1772. James WATSON and Elizabeth Shelton, dau. of David Shelton. Sur. Richard Johnson. Married 1 January 1773 by Rev. William Douglas who says Shilton. p 6

18 December 1804. John WATSON and Nelly Crask. Each is over 21 years of age. Sur. Samuel Watson. p 113

30 September 1783. Ninian WATSON and Sarah Quissenberry. Married by Rev. William Douglas. The Douglas Register p 23

4 August 1788. Randolph WATSON and Lucy Goldsmith. Sur. Philip Reynolds. Married by Rev. John Lasley. p 41

13 March 1809. Benjamin WEBB and Susan Bibb. Sur. Henry Bibb. p 134

10 January 1802. Joseph WEBBER and Jane Ryan. Sur. William Ryan. p 100

4 February 1779. Philip WEBBER and Anna Thomson, dau. of Anna Thomson. Sur. Rhodes Thomson. Wit. Milly Kimbrow and Robert Thomson. p 12

2 July 1784. Henry WEBSTER and Anna Richards. Sur. Joseph Richards. Married 8 July by Rev. William Douglas. p 25

8 November 1802. Shadrach WEBSTER and Salley Attkins. William Attkins gives consent for Salley. Sur. James Tisdale. Wit. Isbil Atkins. p 103

14 December 1790. William WEST and Mary Shelton, dau. of Peter Shelton. Sur. John Austin. Wit. Thomas Shelton. p 53

22 December 1801. Nathaniel WHEELER and Nancey Tisdale, dau. of John Tisdale. Sur. David Tisdale. p 100

5 February 1800. Aaron C. WHITE and Mary A. Thomson, dau. of William Thomson. Sur. William G. Poindexter. Wit. William Chiles and Ann Thomson. Married 6 February by Rev. Richard Ferguson who says Molly. p 92

12 January 1775. Daniel WHITE and Elizabeth McGehee, dau. of William McGehee who consents. Sur. Joseph McGehee. Wit. Austin Luck and William McGehee, Jr. p 9

1 December 1807. George WHITE and Lucy Jackson, dau. of Charles Jackson. Sur. William Jackson. Wit. John N. Christmas. p 126

18 December 1797. Jesse WHITE and Eadith Peers, dau. of Thomas Peers. Sur. Lydall Britton. Wit. William Peers. p 83

__ December 1769. John WHITE and Frances Anderson, dau. of Robert Anderson. Sur. David Anderson. Wit. John Hawkins, Jr. p 2

23 December 1783. John WHITE and Ann Jackson, dau. of Thomas Jackson, Sr. Sur. Thomas Jackson, Jr. Wit. Charles Jackson. Married 25 December by Rev. William Douglas. p 24

18 December 1784. John WHITE and Frances Terry. Sur. Emmanuel Terry. p 27

21 January 1790. John WHITE and Jeanie Crank. Married by Rev. William Douglas. The Douglas Register p 25

21 January 1797. Moses WHITE and Nancy Isbell, dau. of Joseph Isbell. Sur. Robert T. Isbell. Wit. Benjamin C. West. Married 26 January by Rev. Martin Walton. p 80

_____ 1771. Richard WHITE and Lucy Richardson. Sur. George Chapman. p 4

10 June 1782. Capt. Richard WHITE and Mary Meriwether, dau. of Thomas Meriwether. Sur. John Poindexter, Junr. Wit. Nicholas Lewis and Elizabeth Lewis. p 20

21 September 1812. Samuel WHITE and Martha Cosby, dau. of Wingfield Cosby. Sur. Benjamin Cosby. Wit. William C. Goodwin. p 149

8 May 1782. William WHITE, Sr. and Susanna Davis. Sur. John Nelson. Wit. William Winslow. Married 9 May by Rev. William Douglas. p 20

23 December 1806. Hughelet WHITLOCK and Lucy Wright, over 21 years of age. Sur. Thomas Wright. Wit. Edm^d. Banks. p 123

31 January 1797. John WHITLOCK and Nancey Shepherdson. Sur. David Shepheardson. Married 2 February by Rev. John Lasley. p 80

14 February 1810. John WHITLOCK and Sarah Ashlen. Sur. Thomas Porter. p 139

22 January 1799. Nicholas WHITLOCK and Salley Warren. Sur. Bartholomew Warren. Married by Rev. Richard Ferguson. p 88

10 September 1792. Thomas WHITLOCK and Hannah Richardson, dau. of Richard Richardson. Sur. Thomas Brackett. Wit. John Richardson and Ann Richardson. p 59

9 October 1797. Thomas WHITLOCK and Molley Warren. Sur. Bartholomew Warren. Married 12 October by Rev. John Lasley. p 82

8 July 1793. William WHITLOCK, Jr. and Nancey Gunter.
Mrs. Gunter gives consent for Nancey. Sur. William
Whitlock, Sr. p 62

3 February 1773. John WHITTON and Mary McGehee, dau.
of William McGehee. Sur. William Davis. p 6

11 October 1792. James WILKERSON and Charity Stanley.
Solomon Stanley gives consent for Charity. Sur. Ralph
Banks. Wit. John Coates. Married 13 October by Rev.
Richard Pope. p 59

4 June 1789. George WILKINSON and Martha Dickinson,
(Patsy), dau. of Elizabeth Dickinson. Sur. Charles
Fortson (?). Wit. Tarlton B. Luck. Married 7 June
by Rev. John Waller. p 45

20 January 1812. James WILLIAMS and Polly McGehee.
Sur. Dillard McGehee. Married 28 January by Rev. W. E.
Waller. p 146

10 July 1813. James WILLIAMS and Sarah Whitlock, dau.
of Thomas Whitlock. Sur. Stephen Williams. Married
11 July by Rev. John Lasley. p 152

25 February 1793. John WILLIAMS and Elizabeth Ailstock.
Sur. Michael Ailstock, Jr. p 61

12 November 1805. Otho WILLIAMS and Milley Anderson.
Sur. Nathan Anderson. Married by Rev. John B. Magruder of the Methodist Episcopal Church. Returned
21 March 1809. p 117

17 December 1805. Robert WILLIAMS and Sally Wheeler.
Sur. John Wheeler. p 118

8 April 1811. Stephen WILLIAMS and Patsey Whitlock.
Sur. Thomas Whitlock. p 143

2 June 1801. William WILLIAMS and Frances Parrott, dau.
of John Parrott. Sur. William Parrott. p 98

20 November 1810. William WILLIAMS and Jane McGehee,
over 21 years of age, dau. of John McGehee. Sur.
Richard Thomson. p 141

9 November 1791. John WILLS and Lucy M. Barclay, dau.
of James and Mary R. Dickerson. Sur. Lipscomb Crank.
Wit. John L. Boxley. Married 10 November by Rev. John
Waller. p 56

30 May 1812. Benjamin WILTSHIRE and Salley Luck. Sur.
John Luck. Married 3 June by Rev. William Cooke. p 148

28 February 1775. John WILY and Jane Johnson, dau. of William Johnson. Sur. Henry Garrett. John Wily is also written John Willey on the bond and Jane is also written Jean on the bond. p 9

7 March 1767. Anthony WINSTON and Uphan Tate. Sur. Joseph Street. p 10

10 December 1794. Anthony WINSTON and Mary Barrett, dau. of Charles Barrett. Sur. John Peay. p 69

19 June 1810. Bickerton WINSTON, Jr. and Maria Dean Kimbrough. Charles Yancey is Maria's guardian. Sur. William Fleming. Wit. John Edwards. Married 20 June by Rev. William Cooke. p 140

25 November 1811. Horatio G. WINSTON and Clarrisa Morris. Sur. Henry Lawrence. Married 3 December by Rev. John Lasley. p 145

4 December 1780. John WINSTON and Mary Johnson, dau. of Thomas Johnson. Sur. Anderson Thomson. p 16

16 January 1805. John T. WINSTON and Elizabeth G. Anderson. Sur. Francis Anderson. Wit. Benjamin Waddy. Married 17 January by Rev. John Lasley. p 115

15 November 1790. Joseph WINSTON and Rebecca Johnson, dau. of Thomas Johnson, Sr. Sur. Harry Lawrence. p 52

15 April 1811. Nicholas J. WINSTON and Louisa C. Kimbrough. Sur. Charles Yancey. Married 18 April by Rev. William Cooke. p 114

3 December 1811. Philip B. WINSTON and Sarah M. Pendleton, dau. of Henry Pendleton. Sur. Edmund Pendleton. Wit. Barbara O. Pendleton. Married 5 December by Rev. William Cooke. p 145

26 September 1800. William Bobby WINSTON and Nancy Meriwether, dau. of James Meriwether. Sur. Gerard Banks. Wit. A. Banks and Salley Banks. Married 27 September by Rev. Richard Pope. p 94

31 July 1778. Henry WOMACK and Mary Terry. Married by Rev. William Douglas. The Douglas Register p 18

8 March 1804. Christopher WOOD and Elizabeth Wood. Sur. William Wood. Married by Rev. William Ferguson. Returned 1 May 1804. p 111

26 November 1805. Isaac WOOD and Anna R. Bagby. Sur. Nelson Moss. Wit. William Kimbrough. p 117

11 October 1784. James WOOD and Ann Lipscomb. Sur. William Lipscomb. Married 12 October by Rev. William Douglas. p 26

16 January 1788. James WOOD and Sary Johnson, dau. of Matthew Johnson. Sur. William Bibb. Wit. John Bibb and Joseph Johnson. Married 18 January by Rev. John Lasley who says Sarah. p 39

5 November 1807. John WOOD and Mary Bibb, over 21 years of age. Sur. Thomas Bibb. p 126

21 December 1809. John WOOD and Susanna T. Bibb. Sur. Benjamin Bibb. p 138

26 December 1806. Thomas WOOD and Elizabeth Clarke, under age, dau. of Charles Clark. Sur. William R. Tisdale. Wit. William Thompson and Pleasant Cocke. Married 30 December by Rev. William Baskett who says Clark. p 124

30 March 1815. Thomas WOOD and Louisa Gooch, dau. of Stephen Gooch. Sur. Peter M. Daniel. Wit. Ann P. Daniel. Married by Rev. William Y. Hiter. p 158

11 October 1784. William WOOD and Sarah Hall. Sur. William Lipscomb. p 26

10 October 1794. John WOODALL and Sarah Foster. Sur. Stephen Rowe. p 68

6 March 1797. William WOODALL and Sarah Thomasson, orphan. Thomas Greene, John Bowlmer and Anthony Bunch make affadavit that Sarah is 21 years of age. Sur. John Woodall. Wit. Robert Bell. Married 14 March by Rev. John Lasley. p 81

20 August 1789. Thomas WOODGER and Mary Estes, born 20 February 1767, dau. of John and Ursulah Estes. Sur. Abraham Estes. Wit. William Johnson and Thomas Johnson. Thomas Johnson, with whom Mary Estes lived for 21 years, makes Affadavit as to her age. p 45

13 December 1791. Bouth WOODSON and Nancey Shelton, dau. of William Shelton, Sr. Sur. William Woodson. Wit. John Grubbs and Sarah Grubbs. p 57

1 February 1775. Rene WOODSON and Martha Johnson, dau. of David Johnson. Sur. William Johnson. Married 2 February by Rev. William Douglas who says Rene Woodson is of Albemarle County. p 9

12 October 1784. William WOODWARD and Sarah Hall.
Married by Rev. William Douglas. The Douglas Register
p 23

29 December 1778. William WOOLBANKS and Nancy Weatherspoon.
Married by Rev. William Douglas. The Douglas Register
p 18

2 March 1789. Augustine WOOLFOLK and Mrs. Susanna Brown.
Joseph Woolfolk makes affadavit as to Mrs. Brown's age.
Sur. John Duke. Married 6 March by Rev. Charles Hopkins.
p 44

5 July 1786. Joseph WOOLFOLK and Betsey Barnett. Sur.
James Barnett. Married 6 July by Rev. William Douglas
who says Woodfolk. p 32

20 October 1792. Charles WRIGHT and Salley Jarvis. Sur.
James Poindexter. p 59

5 February 1783. John WRIGHT and Fanny Thomason. Married by Rev. William Douglas. The Douglas Register p 22

24 September 1794. John WRIGHT and Elizabeth Walker.
Sur. Clabourn Gooch. p 68

14 July 1790. Joseph WRIGHT and Elizabeth Gooch. Sur.
Claibourne Gooch. Married by Rev. William Douglas.
p 50

14 November 1806. Moses WRIGHT and Febe Bunch. (Phebe?)
Sur. David Bunch. p 122

27 December 1803. Richard WRIGHT and Ann Timberlake.
Sur. Philip Timberlake. Married by Rev. Richard Ferguson. Returned 1 May 1804. p 109

26 January 1789. Absalom YANCEY and Henrietta Nuckolls.
Sur. James Nuckolls. Married 27 January by Rev. John
Waller. p 43

1 December 1807. Charles YANCEY and Mary Edwards, over
21 years of age. Sur. James McAlister. Charles is son
of Augustine Yancey. p 126

10 February 1812. Garland YANCEY and Polly Butler, dau.
of David Butler. Sur. Robert H. Yancey. Wit. N. Thompson. Married 14 February by Rev. William Cooke. p 146

1 November 1773. Joel YANCEY and Barbary Jennings.
Sur. Cosby Duke. p 7

1 December 1802. John YANCEY and Sarah Edwards. Samuel Cole, John's guardian, consents for him. Sur. Joseph Grady. Wit. William Cole and Elizabeth Cosby. p 103

30 December 1796. Richard YANCEY and Mary Walton, dau. of Mary Walton, Sr., who is her guardian. Sur. Richard Nuckolls. Married 1 January 1797 by Rev. James Watkins. p 79

8 October 1779. Stephen YANCEY and Jane Bond, dau. of Thomas Bond. Sur. John Cosby, Junr. Wit. Dudley Harris and John Bond. Married 12 October by Rev. William Douglas who says Jean. p 13

9 January 1775. Tyre YANCEY and Sarah Jennings. Sur. George Lumsden. p 9

20 June 1787. Augustus YANCY and Elizabeth Cole. Sur. ~~Zinvie~~ Tate. p 36

19 July 1785. John YARBROUGH and Mary Dickason, dau. of Robert Dickason. Sur. John Smith. Wit. Higgason Cosby Dickason. p 29

11 April 1791. Samuel E. YEAGER and Mary Hill. Sur. David Hill. Married 12 April by Rev. John Lasley. p 54

2 January 1808. Hackley YOUNG and Frances Peers. Sur. Samuel Cole. Wit. Anderson Peers. p 127

3 March 1797. James YOUNG and Elizabeth Johnson, dau. of Richard Johnson. Sur. William G. Johnson, "brother of the bride". Wit. George Johnson, Jr. p 80

7 August 1781. John YOUNG and Sarah Martin, 31 years of age. Sur. Lawrence Young. Wit. Richard Graves. Married 8 August by Rev. William Douglas. p 17

25 September 1781. Lewis YOUNG and Elizabeth Smith, dau. of Nathan Smith. Sur. Hickason Cosby. Wit. Garland Cosby. Married 27 September by Rev. William Douglas. p 18

21 January 1811. Winston YOUNG and Martha Boxley. Sur. Hackley Young. Wit. Ralph Lane and John Poindexter, Jr. Married 23 January by Rev. W. E. Waller. p 143

I N D E X T O B R I D E S

Badget
| Judah | 13 |
| Judith | 13 |

Badgett
| Elizabeth | 88 |

Bagby
Anna R.	114
Betsy	27
Mildred	99

Baker
Bettsy	18
Elizabeth	50
Frances	81
Mary	109
Nancey	22
Nancy	89
Polley, Jr.	109
Sarah	24
Susanna	71
Temprence	70

Barclay
Elizabeth	40
Lucy M.	113
Mary W.	11

Bark
| Elizabeth | 98 |

Barkley
| Catharine | 11 |

Barnet
| Catherine | 106 |

Barnett
Betsey	116
Elizabeth	34
Nancey	17
Rebecca	38

Barrett
| Elizabeth | 92 |
| Mary | 114 |

Beadles
Leticia	64
Mary W.	17
Nancey	5
Sally	104

Beck
| Frankey | 59 |

Beckley
| Elizabeth | 85 |

Bellomy
| Mary | 15, 106 |

Berry
| Prudence | 10 |

Bettesworth
| Sarah | 57 |

Bibb
Ann	94
Christiana	45
Elizabeth	45
Martha	31, 62
Mary	5, 48, 50, 86, 115
Nancey	48
Nancy	68
Oney	90
Patsy	29, 31, 52
Susan	111
Susanna	70, 98
Susanna T.	115

Bickley
Betsey	89
Caroline Matilda	11
Celia	31
Elizabeth	85
Hendley	50
Jane	16
Mary	72
Matilda	11
Polly	72

Bigger
| Martha | 29 |
| Salley | 75 |

Biggers
Patsey	18
Polly	64
Martha	75
Mary	64
Nancey	30

Black
Sarah 84

Blackwell
Judah 85
Judith 85

Bolton
Mary 41

Bond
Elizabeth 49
Jane 117
Jean 117
Lucy 17
Patsey 63
Patcy 63

Bourn
Elizabeth 68
Mary 4
Susanna 52

Bourne
Hannah 11

Bowe
Olney 79

Bowen
Blendina 37

Bowls
Frances C. 81

Boxley
Catharine 54
Catharine S. 61
Martha 117
Polley 49

Boyd
Elizabeth 91
Mary 23
Mildred 33
Patsey 88

Branham
Polly Ann 69

Brickley
Betcy 89
Elizabeth O. 89

Britton
Elizabeth 79

Broaddus
Elizabeth 12

Broaton
Mary 107

Bronaugh
Peggey 13

Brook
Mary Garrett 21

Brooks
Martha 55
Polley 41
Sarah 68
Susannah 68

Brown
Catharine 85
Martha 69
Marthey 69
Nancy 32
Salley B. 54
Susan 53
Susanna 53
Mrs. Susanna 116

Bullock
Ann 8
Elizabeth 37
Nancey 8
Salley 3

Bunch
Adney 14
Alice 26
Clarysy 15
Dicie 15
Dycie 15
Elizabeth 77, 108
Febe 116
Jeanie 19
Margery 49
Martha 34
Mary 14, 38, 106
Nancy 59
Rhoda 32
Sarah 95
Winny 24

Burgess
    Mildred   2
    Milley   2

Burnley
    Elizabeth   51

Burrus
    Elizabeth   76
    Margaret   30
    Peggy   30
    Sally   4

Burruss
    Mary   68

Burton
    Jane   108
    Sally   51
    Susanna   39

Butler
    Elizabeth   65
    Patsey   45, 51
    Polly   116

Butterworth
    Sarah   57

Byars
    Anne   94
    Elizabeth   17
    Jane   70
    Jean   70
    Martha   50
    Salley   21

Bybe
    Jane   77

Byrd
    Fanny   23

Callis
    Ellenor A.   99
    Lavinia   94

Campbell
    Cassandra   40

Cannaday
    Delphia   109
    Dorothea   32

Cannon
    Betsey   1

Captain
    Nancey   61

Carpenter
    Elizabeth   10
    Frances   46
    Polly   46
    Sally   16
    Sarah   106
    Susanna   52

Carr
    Elizabeth   3
    Mary   74

Carrel
    Nancy   38

Cary
    Mary   71
    Polly   71

Cauthon
    Kitty   60

Cawthon
    Salley L.   96

Cawthorn
    Elizabeth   19

Chace
    Ann   100

Chandler
    Elizabeth   81

Chase
    Sarah   11

Chewning
    Diannah   34
    Jane   82
    Nancey   7, 28
    Patsy   2
    Polly   87

Chiles
    Betsey   17
    Elizabeth   17

Crask (Con't)
    Polly   48

Crawford
    Barbara   14
    Jane   28
    Martha   28
    Polley   55

Crenshaw
    Agnes   37
    Ann   24
    Elizabeth   14, 90
    Jemima   37
    Patsy   106
    Sarah   28
    Susannah   15

Crews
    Agnes   10
    Mary   48
    Nancy   16

Dabney
    Ann Anderson   48
    Ann F.   1
    Ciscely   90
    Mary   47

Dalton
    Polly   90

Daniel
    Jane   8
    Mary M.   57
    Sally   13
    Susanna   3

Darricott
    Cecelia   99
    Cissilla   99

Darvin
    Sarah   105

Dashper
    Polly   86

Davies
    Sarah   47

Davis
    Betsy   5
    Constance   69
    Dorothy   34
    Elizabeth   5
    Frances   39
    Keziah   8
    Mary   50
    Polly   61
    Rhoda   51
    Sarah   99
    Sukey   35
    Susanna   35, 112

Dear
    Frances   51

Depriest
    Elizabeth   95

Desper
    Elizabeth   29
    Nancey   93
    Rosannah   59
    Roseanna   59

Dickason
    Anne   19
    Dolly   85
    Frances   93
    Mary   117
    Sarah   48

Dickenson
    Elizabeth   91
    Maria A.   39

Dickerson
    Elizabeth   71
    Francis   32
    Joannah   71
    Lucey   1
    Sarah   38

Dickinson
    Catharine   42
    Elizabeth   36
    Frances   2
    Martha   113
    Mary   30
    Mary C.   93
    Patsy   113
    Sarah   48

Dickinson (Con't.)
    Sarah   48
    Susanna   12, 81
    Susannah R.   28

Diggs
    Lucy   54
    Polley   96

Douglas
    Elizabeth   34

Douglass
    Elizabeth   33

Drake
    Jane   83

Draper
    Catharine C.   73
    Jane   87

Duke
    Amey   4
    Elizabeth   66, 94
    Jane   43
    Mary   32
    Mary Garland   51
    Nancey   20
    Patsey R.   43
    Patsy Read   44
    Polley   78

Duncan
    Jane   77

Dunn
    Nancey   99
    Ruth   41

Durvin
    Sarah   105

Duval
    Nancy   56
    Patsey   56

Duvall
    Lucy   56

Dyches
    Judith   46

Dyer
    Martha   97

Edds
    Delphia   44

Edrington
    Jane   71

Edwards
    Betsey   102
    Elizabeth   60, 93
    Jenny   59
    Lucy   7
    Malinda   13
    Mary   116
    Milly   38
    Nancy   14, 63
    Polley   54
    Sarah   117
    Salley H.   14

Elmore
    Ann   19

English
    Ann   86

Estes
    Barbara   29
    Mary   115
    Sarah   63

Estis
    Sarah   63

Evans
    Nancey   63

Faris
    Jane   88
    Molly   40
    Sally   18
    Sarah   73

Farish
    Sarah   21

Farmer
    Mary   49

Farrar
    Sally   90
    Sarah   3

Faulkner
    Lucy 66

Ferguson
    Mildred 10

Fielding
    Elizabeth 34

Flannagan
    Mary 24

Fleeman
    Elizabeth 85
    Jane 54

Fleming
    Elizabeth 85, 95
    Lucy 45
    Maria 34
    Mary 66
    Matilda 26
    Mourning 79
    Nancey 41
    Nancy 63, 65
    Patsey 105
    Sarah 22

Fontaine
    Mary Ann 23

Foster
    Fanny 98
    Henrietta 96
    Martha 3
    Mary 14
    Sarah 115

Fox
    Catherine 3
    Caty 3, 56
    Elizabeth 16
    Susanna 110

Freeman
    Elizabeth 80
    Frances 25
    Jane 108
    Nancy 71
    Susanna 6

Freemen
    Sarah 57

Fulcher
    Anne 85
    Mary 27

Fuqua
    Mary G. 7

Gardner
    Ann 78
    Elizabeth 78
    Lucy 1
    Mary 35
    Pheby 32
    Salley 110
    Sarah F. 72
    Temperance 37

Garland
    Ann 62
    Barbara 58
    Barbary 58
    Elander 43
    Henrietta 77
    Judith 92
    Mary 71
    Sarah 71, 77

Garrett
    Elizabeth Ashton 43
    Susanna 58

Garth
    Elizabeth 8
    Patsey 52
    Polley 74
    Sally Perry 51

Gentry
    Elenor B. 3
    Fanney 78
    Frances 98
    Matilda 84
    Milley 7
    Nancey 108
    Nancy 6, 89

Gibbens
    Sarah 92

Gibson
    Ann 17
    Barbara 35
    Catharine 65

Gibson (Con't.)
Frances	30
Henrietta	16
Lucy	39
Susanna	105
Theodosia	57

Gilbert
Elizabeth	86
Polley	85
Salley	24

Gizage
Christian	10

Glenn
Polley	103

Going
Agatha	69

Goldsmith
Elizabeth	64
Lucinda	6
Lucy	111
Milley	91

Gooch
Ann P.	25
Elizabeth	29, 76, 99, 116
Jemima	45
Louisa	115
Lovinah	34
Mary	66, 96, 106
Polly	102
Rhoda	99
Susan	21
Uny	32

Goodman
Ann	15
Elizabeth	15
Lucinda	69

Goodrich
Pasience	18

Goodridge
Pasience	18

Goodwin
Barbary	20

Goodwin (Con't.)
Elizabeth	21
Jane	53
Mary	43

Gordon
Elizabeth R.	21
Lucy	38

Gosney
Mary	27

Grady
Frances	11
Molley	74

Grantler
Nancy	44

Graven
Nancy	28

Graves
Amelia	97
Elizabeth	82, 98
Huldah	47
Lucy	81
Lydia	43
Mary	110
Milley	110
Moley	5
Nancy	102
Sarah	44
Susanna	47
Susannah	19
Susan P.	47

Gray
Anna	89
Sally	4
Sarah	4

Grayson
Mary	92

Green
Lucy	92
Martha	44
Molley	7

Gregson
Elizabeth	76

Grimstead
  Mildred 93

Grinstead
  Mary 33

Groom
  Elizabeth 31
  Jane 92
  Nancy 8
  Patsey 40
  Polly 90

Grubbs
  Betsey 59
  Martha 104
  Mary 79
  Mildred 47
  Milly 47
  Nancy 79
  Salley 33

Gunnell
  Elizabeth 26
  Mary 66
  Nancy 61

Gunter
  Nancey 113
  Permelia 109

Haines
  Mary 40

Haley
  Sarah 31
  Tabitha 31

Hall
  Barbara 61
  Frances 65
  Rebecca 26
  Sarah 108, 115, 116

Haly
  Delany 31

Hambleton
  Elizabeth 89
  Mourning 82
  Sarah 109
  Salley 53
  Salley H. 53

Hampton
  Sally 47

Hancock
  Mary 15
  Nancey 101

Hanes
  Elizabeth Sharp 91
  Frances S. 22
  Mary 60

Hansford
  Milly 103

Harger
  Frankey 27

Harper
  Frances 34
  Mary 46
  Nancy 110
  Patsy 47

Harris
  Amelia 23
  Ann 23
  Barbara 48
  Barbara Overton 110
  Betsey 13
  Catharine 69
  Charlotte 28
  Elizabeth 12, 13,
    32, 34, 35, 109
  Jemima 50, 88
  Lucy 22
  Mariah 49
  Martha B. 69
  Mary 89, 101
  Molly 36
  Nancey 36
  Nancy 6, 21
  Polly 78
  Rebecca T. 10
  Sarah 95
  Salley 96
  Savary 109
  Susannah 101

Harrison
  Judith 44

Hart
    Judith   13

Hatton
    Polly   101

Haywood
    Nancey   83

Henderson
    Ann   52
    Jenny   90

Hendley
    Polley   10

Henley
    Judith   55
    Polley   10

Henson
    Polley   27
    Sarah   9

Herndon
    Sarah   43

Hester
    Elizabeth   76
    Mary M.   67

Hickason
    Charity   96

Higgason
    Frances   24

Hill
    Ann   51
    Judith   36
    Lydda   45
    Lyddia   44
    Mary   117

Hinchey
    Salley   14

Hinchie
    Polley   11

Hix
    Unity   101

Hogard
    Barbara   38

Hoggard
    Ann   69
    Barbara   38
    Delilah   57

Holland
    Ann   56
    Betty   87
    Dolley   75
    Frankey   62
    Judith   42
    Mary   18, 55

Hollins
    Ann   56
    Catharine   37
    Jane T.   52
    Sally   86

Holt
    Elizabeth   56

Homes
    Elizabeth   29

Hope
    Elizabeth   20
    Frances   59
    Martha H.   56

Hopkins
    Elizabeth   9
    Mary   46

Houchins
    Joice   43

Hubbard
    Elizabeth   92
    Mary   62
    Nancey   19

Hudson
    Elizabeth   62

Hughes
    Molley Anderson   30
    Suckey   25
    Sucky   29
    Susanna   67

Hughs
Susanna   67

Hughson
Elizabeth   110

Humble
Ann   9

Humbles
Keziah   62

Humphrey
Betsey   74
Elizabeth   74
Frances   26
Lucy   100
Nancey   78
Rebekah T.   60

Humphreys
Martha   67

Hunter
Elizabeth   45, 57
Jeanie   66
Lucy   58
Martha   81
Mary   84
Milley   54
Nancey   1
Nancy   1, 78

Hutson
Jeanie   54
Sarah   87

Inscip
Charlotte   88

Isbell
Elizabeth   11
Nancy   112
Polly   108

Jackson
Agnes A.   56
Ann   19, 112
Elizabeth   12
Lucy   111
Mary   95
Polley   95

Jacobs
Elizabeth   13

Jarvis
Salley   116

Jennings
Barbary   116
Judith   31
Sally   95
Sarah   95, 117

Jerdone
Anne   102
Elizabeth   67
Isabella   74
Mary   83
Sarah   12

Johnson
Alice   51
Ann   26, 38, 56
Ann M.   8
Ann Meriwether   8
Betsey   9
Dorothy   73
Elizabeth   26, 75,
                 108, 117
Elizabeth Barber   30
Elizabeth H.   63
Elizabeth
         Thornton   82
Frances   104
Frances Pope   82
Hannah Edwards   19
Jancy   55
Jane   114
Janey   55
Jean   81, 114
Keziah   57
Lucey   85
Lucy   85
Luraney   20
Luranna   20
Martha   66, 70, 115
Mary   12, 62, 114
Massie   57
Nancey   58
Nancy   93
Patsy   78
Rebecca   114
Roseanna   33
Salley   78

Leonard
Mary	43
Peggie	96
Peggy	91

Lewis
Betsey	100
Elizabeth A.	44

Linch
Frances	48

Linney
Margarett	4

Lipscomb
Ann	115
Annes	26
Annis	7
Dianah	101
Elizabeth	64, 91
Frances	93
Fanny	104, 105
Judith	107
Lucy	87, 91
Martha	59
Mary	63
Poley	110
Polley	49
Salley	107
Sarah	86
Susan	8

Locker
Henney	88

Long
Dorothea	14

Longest
Elizabeth	71

Lovell
Elizabeth	36

Lowry
Mildred	39

Luck
Crosby C.	5
Elizabeth	95
Molly (2)	35
Salley	113

Lumsden
Nancey	5

Lunsden
Frances	67

McAllister
Elizabeth	4, 21, 50

McCallester
Polly	51

McDaniel
Jane	58
Nancy	84

McGehee
Barbara	45
Betsey	41
Easter	72
Eliza	53
Elizabeth	22, 53, 111
Jane	113
Judith	106
Liddia	101
Lucy	18, 52
Lydia	72
Mary	102, 113
Mary Ann	5
Mary H.	11
Matilda	97
Mitilda	97
Nancey	22
Nancy	32
Patsey	55
Polley	83
Polly	113
Rebecca	5
Sarah	10, 46
Susanna	17

Madison
Ann P.	27

Maddison
Eliza C.	78
Sally	41

Maifield
Agnes	52

Moore
    Susanna   14

Moorman
    Mary   98

Morgan
    Rishey   100

Morris
    Amy   48
    Carolina Matilda   33
    Clarrisa   114
    Elizabeth   2, 37, 55
    Nancy P.   68
    Polley   55, 104
    Sally   10, 35

Morton
    Sarah   87

Moss
    Dianah   94
    Dolly   8
    Nancey   41
    Rebecca   59

Murphy
    Ann   48

Napper
    Elizabeth   42
    Patty   12

Nelson
    Ann   105
    Elizabeth   70
    Frances A.   25
    Mary   45
    Polly   45

Newton
    Sarah   95

Nichols
    Ann   48

Norman
    Franky   18

Nuckolds
    Elizabeth   101
    Mary   4

Nuckolls
    Elizabeth G.   67
    Henrietta   116
    Jane   50
    Nancy   50

Overton
    Ann   21
    Fanny G.   106
    Jemima Ann   7
    Mary   76
    Sarah   20
    Sarah G.   99
    Sarah M.   99

Overstreet
    Sally   49

Parish
    Cynthia F.   80
    Fanny   102
    Martha   43

Parrish
    Doney   62
    Eliza   89
    Frances   45
    Mary   37
    Susanna   104

Parrott
    Frances   113

Parsons
    Elley   80
    Sally   96

Pass
    Susanna   84

Paterson
    Elizabeth   61

Payne
    Nancey   7
    Sally   25, 31

Peay
    Polley   53

Peed
    Betsey   79
    Elizabeth   79

Sanders
Elizabeth 34
Rietta 24

Sandidge
Cadance 42
Martha 105
Marry 28
Mary 28
Nancey 27

Sansom
Elizabeth 27

Sansum
Catharine Dorrell 27
Mary 2
Sarah 21

Saunders
Elizabeth 34
Margaret 40

Seargeant
Nancy 86
Patsy, Junr. 37
Polly 10

Seay
Salley 100

Sergeant
Salley 15

Serjeant
Hithie 8

Settle
Rosa 41

Shackleford
Mary 4

Sharp
Anne 109
Frances 23
Mary O. 108
Susannah 65
Temperance 81

Shelton
Betsey 23
Elizabeth 1, 110
Judith 79

Shelton (Con't.)
Lucy 6
Martha 65
Mary 111
Nancey 115
Salley 45
Sarah 99
Susanna 33

Shepard
Polley 35
Polly 87

Shepherd
Lucy 39

Shepherdson
Elizabeth 91
Nancey 112

Shields
Elizabeth 71

Shilton
Elizabeth 110

Shirley
Barshaba 68

Sims
Ann 1
Babby 80
Elizabeth 12, 48
Nancey 15
Polley 97
Rebecca 16
Rhoda 16
Salley 60
Susanna 46

Simson
Mary 81

Slater
Elizabeth 85

Slayden
Sarah 63

Sledd
Fanny 38

Smith
Ann 58, 83

Young (Con't.)
      Elizabeth Y.   103
      Frances   71
      Judith   18
      Nancey L.   75
      Kitty   44
      Patty   28
      Sarah   55

www.ingramcontent.com/pod-product-compliance
Lightning Source LLC
Chambersburg PA
CBHW021831020426
42334CB00014B/580